What Should Teachers Know About Technology?

Perspectives and Practices

A volume in
Research Methods for Educational Technology
Series Editors: Walter Heinecke and Kirk Knestis, *University of Virginia*

Research Methods for Educational Technology Series

Series Editors:
Walter F. Heinecke, *University of Virginia*
Kirk Knestis, *University*

Methods of Evaluating Educational Technology
Walter F. Heinecke and Laura Blasi

What Should Teachers Know About Technology?: Perspectives and Practices
Yong Zhao

What Should Teachers Know About Technology?

Perspectives and Practices

Edited by

Yong Zhao
Michigan State University

INFORMATION AGE PUBLISHING

80 Mason Street • Greenwich, Connecticut 06830 • www.infoagepub.com

Library of Congress Cataloging-in-Publication Data

What should teachers know about technology : perspectives and practices
/ edited by Yong Zhao.
    p. cm. – (Research methods for educational technology)
Includes bibliographical references (p.   ).
 ISBN 1-59311-037-5 (hardcover) – ISBN 1-59311-036-7 (pbk.)
1. Educational technology. 2. Teachers–Training of. I. Zhao, Yong,
1965- II. Research methods for educational technology (Unnumbered)
LB1028.3.W44 2003
371.33–dc21

                                          2003005926

Printed in the United States of America

CONTENTS

SERIES EDITORS' PREFACE

> The new technology has the potentiality for improvement that does not reside in the old. But it is only a means. The effectiveness of the means depends on the skill of those who employ them. It is therefore important to consider not only the education goals sought but also what is actually involved in learning and teaching. (Trow, 1963, p. 17)

It might have been written yesterday but, in fact, the year that this passage was published, John F. Kennedy was fatally shot as he rode through Dealey Plaza, in downtown Dallas, Texas. George Wallace was sworn in as the Governor of Alabama—vowing in his inaugural address, "Segregation now; segregation tomorrow; segregation forever!" The Beatles topped the British rock charts with "Please, Please Me" and first hit the U.S. charts with "From Me to You." Mickey Mantle and Willie Mays each signed baseball contracts worth $100,000 and James Whittaker became the first American to successfully reach the summit of Mount Everest. Boeing celebrated the first flight of its 727 airliner and the home video recorder was first demonstrated at the BBC Studios in London.

It has been 40 years since then and the face of American politics has changed, the Beatles have sold millions of records and two have lost their lives, professional ball players now sign contracts worth millions of dollars per year, and even adventure athletes like mountain climbers attract lucrative promotional agreements. Technology has been redefined, advancing well beyond William Clark Trow's (1963) definition of the word. To him, "new technology" meant educational television and "teaching machines" (p. 90)—advances that, in their time, held great potential to revolutionize education.[1] However, what Trow reminds us was true then is still true today:

What Should Teachers Know About Technology?: Perspectives and Practices, pages vii–xi
Copyright © 2003 by Information Age Publishing
All rights of reproduction in any form reserved.

the effective integration of technology in education depends on people, teachers and students, interpreting technology and then acting on those interpretations.

> A list might be drawn up of conditions that need remedying, including class size, promotion policy, reading instruction, equipment, teaching load, curriculum offerings, and so on. The usual procedure is to tinker with the most troublesome problem, such as overcrowding, and add a new wing, a new course, or a new teacher, or if the bond issue passed, even a new building, perhaps one that except for certain new building materials would have been a modern marvel in 1930. These may be good temporary solutions, but there is a danger that as a consequence things will not be much better than they were before (Trow, 1963, p. 119).

It might seem as though the issues have not changed significantly in the last four decades. We are still negotiating solutions to challenges, including our relationship with technology in education settings—described by editor Yong Zhao early in this volume as the "application of human knowledge to practical problems." We are still trying to adequately define technological literacy, still working to effectively train teachers to use technology in their work, and still wrestling with the problem of how best to help future teachers learn about technology.

What then has changed? Though not exclusively a modern issue, the accountability movement and emphasis on high-stakes testing, catalyzed by the publication of *A Nation at Risk* (*A nation at risk: The imperative for educational reform*, 1983), has increased the pressure on teachers and school administrators. The challenges of educational practice, if anything, seem greater now, so how can we hope to ensure that our current uses of technology in education have more lasting impact than did the "teaching machines"? Perhaps hope comes in the form of collective experience, with new perspectives resulting from research into the application of instructional technology, and from the willingness to revisit some very fundamental questions:

> Perhaps the greatest advantage accruing from the advance of technology into the realm of education is the occasion it provides for careful scrutiny of educational objectives and techniques. Just what is education trying to do? And what are the best ways of doing it? (Trow, 1963, p. 7)

In the first volume of this series we attempted to explore the evaluation of educational technology. We determined that certain fundamental questions must be asked and answered such as: What is the definition of technology? What is the purpose of education and how are teaching and learning defined? What is the definition of "effective" technology integration? In this volume of Research Methods for Educational Technology, Yong Zhao of Michigan State University, focuses on what teachers know about technology and takes a significant step in clarifying some of these issues. Zhao and the authors in the volume keep us focused on the importance of the relationship between pedagogy and technology. Zhao introduces a new concept: Pedagogical content technology knowledge. The authors also highlight the relationship between values and beliefs about technology and teaching. For instance efficiency-oriented perspectives may lead to teaching as delivery of discrete bits of information and skills and technology as a tool to reinforce these practices. Perspectives promoting quality or excellence may spur images of teachers as facilitators and students as co-constructors of knowledge and technology as a tool in the process of teaching higher order thinking and content-oriented process skills. In an era of high stakes accountability we risk constraining our definition of effective technology use to those practices leading solely to increases in standardized test scores. Zhao's volume helps us keep our eye on the ball by focusing not on what teachers should learn but how they should learn about the complexity of technology integration.

Zhao revisits the rise in importance of information and communication technologies (or ICT) and examines them from a variety of perspectives. He reminds us that students' access to information has increased to a previously unheard-of level, as the number of schools connected to the Internet almost tripled between 1994 and 2000. As a result of this and other influences, technology competency is increasingly viewed as a necessary element of a teacher's professional qualifications.

Perhaps most importantly, Zhao illuminates the transition from a paradigm that wondered whether technology had a role in education to one that honestly expects that we can explain what that role is. By extension, it then becomes necessary to understand and define what constitutes a technologically competent teacher. It is tempting to simply define the technology skills, processes, knowledge and concepts that we think are necessary but we must really start by attempting to answer, in the context of the computer-enabled classroom, Trow's (1963) question: "What is actually involved in learning and teaching?" (p. 17).

Zhao begins this process by exploring the relationships between problems and the qualities of an object that define the kind of tool it can be, making it clear that clarifying the problem is therefore a critical first step. Without establishing this in advance, the qualities of an effective tool and the skills necessary to use it are illusive, and computers become a solution in search of a problem. To effectively use a tool, we must understand the attributes, biases and propensities inherent in its design. We are also well advised to remember that functional knowledge of technology is not only foundational to future use, it also helps us identify new problems that computers might help educators solve.

We also must understand the physical and social contexts in which the teaching-learning process takes place and consider carefully the interactive aspects of processes and contexts. Knowledge of technology is firmly situated in the times and settings where technology-supported teaching and learning take place. Well-equipped teachers should be able to decide, in a variety of situations, when technology tools are appropriate to their problems and when they are not.

Zhao and his colleagues also make it clear that conceptual frameworks, typologies and taxonomies can help clarify our understanding of both problems and the tools that we might apply to address them. Most simply, we might categorize computer technologies by the type of problems to which they can be applied. Technology skills and understandings might also be usefully aligned with domains of knowledge immediately relevant to teachers, like pedagogy and content area knowledge.

The challenge of course is assuring that all educators understand these things. Trow (1963) suggests that...

> It will no doubt be some time before teacher-training institutions can give their students the benefits that experience with instruction by the new media can bring. But meanwhile, their graduates in increasing numbers will be securing positions in schools where the new technology is already at various stages of development. The first step has already been taken in a number of institutions, that of adding new courses and workshops, primarily for teachers in service, to train them in the use of the new media and to furnish consulting services. (p. 168)

This is not likely to be an effective approach, however, adding to already-packed teacher preparation programs. Readers will find that the authors of this volume recommend this course of action only if specific conditions are provided, generally suggesting instead that technology be routinely integrated into the other coursework. Though more challenging to implement, this approach makes unavoidable demands on faculty members, and there exists a risk that technology understandings can be lost in other content or simply ignored.

It is necessary that teacher educators appreciate the complexity of both educational technology knowledge and the mechanisms through which it is acquired, if we are to realize the promise of a theme that re-emerges in the latter portion of this volume:

> The new media will not be particularly effective so long as they remain mere aids or adjuncts, an intrusion, a fifth wheel to the educational conveyance. The new parts need to be integrated into a man-machine system, and this

requires clear-cut readjustments in organization and procedure. The required changes may take a little time but they are well within the range of feasibility. (Trow, 1963, p 180)

Examining the relationship among pedagogy, content, and technology is a critical challenge for educational technology and this volume contributes significantly to this endeavor.

—Walter F. Heinecke
Kirk Knestis

Center for Technology and Teacher Education
Curry School of Education
University Of Virginia

NOTE

1. "Teaching machines," known alternately as "learning machines," "tutoring machines" or "auto-instruction devices," were mechanical, electro-mechanical or electronic instruments designed to provide "programmed learning." Students were presented with an organized set of questions, a mechanism with which to provide responses and the provision for immediate feedback to the learner, indicating whether his answer was correct or incorrect (Trow, 1963, p. 90).

REFERENCES

A nation at risk: The imperative for educational reform. (1983). Washington, D.C.: National Commission on Excellence in Education.

Trow, W. C. (1963). *Teacher and technology: New designs for learning.* New York: Meredith Publishing.

INTRODUCTION

There is a growing concern among the public that our teachers are not adequately prepared to reap the educational benefits of the ostensibly powerful and expensive information and communication technologies that have been pouring into our schools. The well-publicized gap between access to and utilization of modern technologies such as computers (Becker, 2000; Cuban, 1999, 2001; Loveless, 1996) has created a sense of urgency between policy makers and teacher educators, as well as teachers and school administrators, that we must do something to ensure that all our teachers are proficient in their use of information technologies as educational tools (International Society for Technology in Education, 2000; National Council for Accreditation of Teacher Education, 1997; U.S. Congress Office of Technology Assessment, 1995; U.S. Department of Education, 2000). Consequently, virtually all states have added technology proficiency to their teacher licensing requirements. The federal government has created grant programs specifically for the preparation of technologically fluent teachers. Accreditation agencies have added technology to their list of essential elements that a teacher education program must include. In response, teacher education programs and school districts have invested heavily in educational technology courses or professional development efforts that aim at helping teachers, both pre-service and in-service, to learn how to use technology as a pedagogical tool.

This collection of articles deals with two critical issues facing teacher educators regarding technology: What should teachers know about technology and how to effectively prepare them to know that? Defining what teachers should know about technology is no easy task for a number of rea-

What Should Teachers Know About Technology?: Perspectives and Practices, pages xiii–xviii
Copyright © 2003 by Information Age Publishing
All rights of reproduction in any form reserved.

sons. First, technology is a very broad and ill-defined term (Ohler, 1999). It can mean any application of human knowledge to solve practical problems. It includes not only mechanical artifacts, but also procedures and practices. Even when technology is interpreted as only mechanical objects, the range of objects is almost inexhaustible: from simple things such as the overhead projector and pencil to complex systems such as the computer and Internet. Even when we further narrow technology down to the computer, the list of things teachers need to know is still not easy to create.

The second issue has to do with the appropriate level of abstraction and attributes of technology. All technology can be examined (taught) at different levels, including internal structures (how it works), functions (what it does), utilities (what problems it solves), and implications (what it means). Take e-mail, a computer application that is often considered common and simple, as an example. E-mail can be considered in terms of the underlying computing processes that enable it, its functionality, how it can be used in teaching, or the legal, ethical, and practical consequences of electronic communication. This means that decisions must be made regarding whether to teach about hardware and software that enables e-mail, network protocols, pedagogical uses; the social and psychological issues associated with e-mail use by students and teachers; or both.

The third issue is that technology is constantly changing. New technology emerges on a daily basis. The half-life of technology has become extremely short, making it very difficult to decide what knowledge may be useful after teachers complete their education and enter the classroom. And finally, given that most teacher education programs are already packed with required course work and field experiences, it is difficult to add one more component into the existing curriculum. Thus, it becomes critical to identify and define what technology knowledge would be useful for teachers and would at the same time be teachable.

This book offers a comprehensive view of the prominent perspectives on technology literacy for teachers and current practices in preparing teachers to be technologically literate. In the first chapter, Yong Zhao unpacks the question of what teachers should know about technology, into four fundamental issues–the first being what teachers should know *about* technology in order to use it. Zhao proposes that there is a distinction between technological artifacts and technological functions. He argues that technology implies an inseparable relationship between a problem and a solution. In order to use a technology, users must be able to understand both the problem (or problems) it is intended to solve and its qualities that form the solution. He also suggests that since teachers are often not the inventors of technologies, their problems are often not exactly the same as those preconceived by the inventors. Thus teachers need to be able to reinterpret technological functions in their own context, so as to make the problem-solution connection. The second issue Zhao raises in this chapter is what technologies teachers should know to support their teaching. He discusses this issue within the greater context of teacher knowledge and proposes a number of ways to use teachers' pedagogical activities as a framework to select the technologies that should form the core of teacher technology knowledge. The third issue Zhao discusses is the amount of technology teachers should know, as he outlines a three-level proficiency model of technology knowledge: mechanical, meaningful, and generative. Finally, Zhao discusses in detail ways to effectively teach technology to teachers. He analyzes the relative advantages and shortcomings of two common approaches to preparing technologically proficient teachers.

Chapter 2 by Paul Conway and Yong Zhao discusses how policy makers view teachers in relation to technology, and investigates implications for defining what teachers should know about technology. Specifically, this chapter reports the findings of a study examining how state educational technology plans portray teachers in relation to technology. State technology plans are state-level policy documents that spell out missions and needs in educational technology of a state, as they identify and prioritize areas of investment and present strategies of implementation. Through the examination technology plans for 18 of the United States, the authors found that the views of teachers have been moved from that of Luddites to gatekeepers to adopters to designers. This shift of view has significant implications for discussions about what teachers should know about technology. As designers, the authors argue, teachers need to have a much more flexible and contextualized understanding of technology than previously conceived.

Chapter 3 continues the discussion of the policy perspective on what teachers should know about technology. In this chapter, Zhao, Kendall, and Tan report findings of an analysis of national and state technology standards for teachers in the United States. In recent years, a number of technology standards have been developed to guide teacher education institutions in their efforts to teach teachers how to use technology. These standards now serve as the primary policy documents that define technology knowledge for teachers and, although they share some similarities, they also have significant differences. This chapter summarizes and critiques the content of these standards, and discusses their implications for preparing teachers to use technology.

Chapter 4 by Levin and Bruce takes a different perspective on this issue, centering on technology as media for learning. Based on a taxonomy of educational technology, this learner-centered perspective emphasizes that the technology knowledge expected of teachers should be derived from what they do with technology to support student learning. The authors suggest that technology can be classified into four categories in terms of its function to support students' natural impulses to learn and grow–media for inquiry, media for construction, media for communication, and media for expression. In order for technology to be effectively and wisely used, teachers need to understand technology in the context of learning. Their understanding of technology should not start from hardware, software, or even computing concepts, but from the functions that may support the learner's impulse to interact, explore, express, and construct.

Urban-Lurain offers yet another perspective on teacher technology knowledge in Chapter 5. Approaching this issue from a computer science view, he suggests "Fluency with Information Technology" (or FITness) as a possible way to conceptualize teacher technology knowledge, emphasizing a flexible understanding of computing and other technologies. Teachers, like all others who live in an information society, need to be fluent with information technology (FIT). What teachers need to know are fundamental computing concepts so that they may adapt to and learn a variety of applications. Based on a large-scale study, the author identifies key computing concepts that define FITness.

While Chapters 2 through 5 focus on the different perspectives on what teachers should know about technology, the last three chapters are case studies of how to effectively prepare teachers to use technology. In Chapter 6, Rosaen and Bird report on an in-depth study of an integrative approach to preparing teachers to use technology, that emphasizes the "usefulness" of technology for teachers and teacher educators. Instead of explicit and direct instruction, teachers learn about appropriate uses of technology through authentic learning experiences, in which technology is used. In this case, through engagement in constructing technology-supported portfolios, pre-service teachers learn to understand how technology can be used to solve authentic problems in teacher education. The authors carefully documented the process, which can serve as an example for other teacher educators and teacher education programs. Their findings about teacher candidates' perceptions and interpretations of software and assignments, engagement in the portfolio process, and necessary support structures have practical and theoretical implications in our quest to define what teachers should know, and to effectively help teachers know about technology.

While Rosaen and Bird's study was situated in teacher education courses for pre-service teachers, the study reported by Mishra and Koehler in Chapter 7 took place in educational technology courses for in-service teachers. "Learning by design" is examined as a powerful way of teaching teachers to use technology as, in their view, technology is best learned by engaging learners in actual uses of technology. In this chapter, the authors describe in detail the "design approach" and reflect on their experiences applying it in preparing teachers to use technology.

The last chapter by Margerum-Leys and Marx describes knowledge of educational technology as it is acquired, used, and shared between a group of pre-service teachers and the experienced in-service teachers with whom they worked during their student teaching experience. A goal of this case study is to describe the knowledge held by the participants in a way that addresses the inherent complexity and situate nature of knowledge. To do this, the authors frame their conception around Shulman's (1987) general framework for teacher knowledge. Their findings suggest the importance of authentic experiences for teachers to acquire technology knowledge.

In summary, the chapters in this book present a variety of perspectives on teacher technology knowledge, and practices that seem to be effective in helping teachers acquire that knowledge. Although their perspectives may differ, the authors seem to point out a number of common themes. First, the definition of what teachers should know about technology seems to move away from a simple mechanical understanding toward more situated and contextualized knowledge of how technology interacts with teaching and learning. In other words, what a teacher should know about technology should be defined based on their professional activities. Second, teachers are viewed as more active in the process of using technology, as they actively interpret and reinterpret the values and uses of technology in their own context. Third, effective approaches to preparing technologically proficient teachers should engage teachers in authentic uses of technology to solve teaching and learning problems.

—**Yong Zhao**
East Lansing, Michigan
September 2002

ACKNOWLEDGMENTS

This book evolved out of a symposium presented at the 2000 annual meeting of the American Educational Research Association in Seattle, Washington. Earlier versions of Chapters 2, 3, 4, and 5 were presented at this conference. A version of Chapter 1 was presented at the International Symposium on Teacher Education in Nanjing, China in November 2001. Chapter 8 is published in the *Journal of Educational Computing Research* (volume 26, issue 4) and is reprinted with permission from the publisher.

The development and production of this book depended on the talent and hard work of many colleagues. I want to first thank all the authors for their insights, efforts, and support. I am grateful to series editor Walter Heinecke and his very able assistant Kirk Knestis, for their guidance, assistance, and patience. I must also thank Rick Banghart for the many conversations we have had about technology in education, teachers and technology, and technology and life in general. In preparation for this book, I also benefitted a great deal from conversations with Andrew Henry, Meg Ropp, Patrick Dickson, Robert Floden, and Tom Bird. Finally I am indebted to my wife and children. Without their understanding and support, this book would not even have been attempted.

REFERENCES

Becker, H.J. (2000). Who's wired and who's not: Children's access to and use of computer technology. *The Future of Children, 10*(2), 44–75.

Cuban, L. (1999, August 4). The technology puzzle: Why is greater access not translating into better classroom use? *Education Week,* pp. 68, 47.

Cuban, L. (2001). *Oversold and underused: Computers in Schools 1980-2000.* Cambridge, MA: Harvard University Press.

International Society for Technology in Education. (2000). *National educational technology standards for teachers.* Eugene, OR: Author.

Loveless, T. (1996). Why aren't computers used more in schools? *Educational Policy, 10*(4), 448–467.

National Council for Accreditation of Teacher Education. (1997). *Technology and the new professional teacher: Preparing for the 21st century classroom.* Washington, DC: Author.

Ohler, J. (1999). *Taming the beast: Choice and control in the electronic jungle.* Bloomington, IN: TECHNOS.

Shulman, L. S. (1987). Knowledge and teaching: Foundations of the new reform. *Harvard Educational Review, 57*(1), 1–22.

U.S. Congress, Office of Technology Assessment. (1995). *Teachers and technology: Making the connection* (OTA-EHR-616). Washington, DC: Office of Technology Assessemnt.

U.S. Department of Education. (2000). *E-learning: Putting a world-class education at the fingertips of all children: The national educational technology plan.* Washington, DC: Author.

CHAPTER 1

WHAT TEACHERS NEED TO KNOW ABOUT TECHNOLOGY?

Framing the Question

Yong Zhao

INTRODUCTION

Modern information and communication technologies (ICTs) are rapidly entering schools in the hope that these expensive tools will improve student learning, increase teachers' productivity, and prepare our children to live and work in an information society, where ICTs play an essential and ubiquitous role. The ratio of students to instructional computers connected to the Internet in American public schools, for example, dropped from 12:1 to 7:1 in a matter of two years between 1998 and 2000. The percentage of American public schools connected to the Internet increased from 35% in 1994 to 98% in 2000 (Cattagni & Farris, 2001). The increased presence of ICTs in schools has been accompanied by increased demand for teachers who are capable of using these supposedly powerful tools so as to realize their educational potentials. Technology competency has been increasingly viewed as a necessary element of a teacher's professional qual-

What Should Teachers Know About Technology?: Perspectives and Practices, pages 1–14
Copyright © 2003 by Information Age Publishing

ifications (The CEO Forum on Education and Technology, 1999; National Council for Accreditation of Teacher Education, 1997; U.S. Congress Office of Technology Assessment, 1995). Today, as attested to by (a) the technology requirements issued by government teacher licensing agencies, (b) teacher education program accreditation agencies, (c) international professional organizations, (d) technology professional development programs initiated by schools, and (e) the addition and expansion of the technology component in teacher education programs, it is no longer a question whether teachers should know something about technology.

The question has changed from whether to what. In order for school districts and licensing agencies to assess whether practicing teachers are technologically competent, for teacher educators to prepare technologically competent teachers, and for all teachers to develop their own technology proficiency, it is necessary to have a good understanding of what teachers need to know about technology. The quest for such an understanding is as challenging a task as is the attempt to understand what makes effective teachers and efficient teaching (Borko & Putnam, 1996; Calderhead, 1996; Edelfelt & Raths, 1999; Gage, 1963; Richardson, 2001; Shulman, 1987; Travers, 1973; Wittrock, 1986).

Difficult though it may be, many people have embarked on this journey. This collection of papers reports findings from some of the efforts to define teachers' technology competencies that have been undertaken at multiple levels and from various perspectives. It is hoped that what is learned from these pioneering efforts will help light the paths to follow, and dead ends to avoid, in the future. In this essay, I discuss the major issues considered by the included chapters with the intention to develop a framework for understanding teachers' technology knowledge.

FROM ARTIFACT TO TOOL: WHAT DO TEACHERS NEED TO KNOW TO USE TECHNOLOGY?

When considering what teachers need to know about technology in order to use it, I found the following story told by the wise man Aesop extremely enlightening and relevant:

> A thirsty crow found a pitcher with some water in it, but so little was there that, try as she might, she could not reach it with her beak, and it seemed as though she would die of thirst within sight of the remedy. At last she hit upon a clever plan. She began dropping pebbles into the pitcher, and with each pebble the water rose a little higher until at last it reached the brim, and the knowing bird was enabled to quench her thirst. (Aesop, 1912, p. 17)

In this story, Aesop illustrates the essence of technology. The pebbles were simply irrelevant physical objects until four things happened: (a) the crow felt thirsty, (b) the crow saw a pitcher of water, (c) the water is too low for her to reach, and (d) she realized that the pebbles could be used to raise the water level. Connecting the pebbles to her need for water, the crow turns irrelevant objects into a tool, a technology—a solution to her problem. At this moment, the pebbles are no longer pebbles but a powerful tool for the thirsty crow. What turns the pebbles into a tool is the crow's knowledge of the relationship between a problem and the quality of an object.

Teachers' uses of technology are certainly more complex than the thirsty crow's using pebbles to help her get to the water but they have some striking similarities. While computers and the Internet are much more sophisticated and created more purposefully than Aesop's pebbles, they are as irrelevant and useless as pebbles until they are used to solve a problem. Unless they are used, computers remain a man-made object, or an artifact. They only become a tool, a means to an end, when they are connected to a problem.

Admittedly, technology is different from natural physical objects such as the crow's pebbles, in that they are made to solve practical problems. However, a technological object is quite often other people's solutions to other people's problems. A word processor application is the software developer's solution to the perceived problems of composing and editing texts. It only becomes a tool for a specific user when she uses it to solve her problems of composing and editing texts. In order to turn the word processor application from an artifact into a tool, the user must first know that she needs to compose and edit, and then realize that the word processor can help her compose and edit. Since most technologies introduced to schools have not been developed as educational tools—tools that solve problems teachers face in their work—very often they remain expensive artifacts rather than useful tools because teachers do not consider them solutions to their problems. This is one of the main reasons that most school technologies have been unused or underused (Becker, 1999; Cuban, 1986, 1999, 2001; Loveless, 1996; Smerdon, Cronen, Lanahan, Anderson, Iannotti, & Angeles, 2000).

A technology has its built-in functions. These functions represent the developer's knowledge of the connection between a problem and a solution. In other words, technology is a knowledge system (Hickman, 1990). Thus, technology is not neutral or unbiased. Rather, it has its own propensities, biases, and inherent attributes (Bromley, 1998; Bruce, 1993). Its inherent attributes or functions suggest to its prospective users what problems a particular technology might solve. For example, the functions of an e-mail program make a strong suggestion that it is designed to solve communication problems through electronic means. Hence, for teachers to use a technology, they need to know its inherent functions. Knowledge of the functions of a technology helps teachers not only make the connection between the technology and existing problems but also identify new problems.

However, as mentioned earlier, the problems identified by the developer may not be the same problems that teachers face, therefore the built-in functions of a technology are often considered irrelevant by teachers unless they are presented as solutions to educational problems. For instance, most word processor applications today have the function for embedding annotations in the document. This function represents a solution to the problem of leaving notes within a document but the problem is not necessarily an educational one. Until it is connected to educational problems such as inserting comments into student writings or having students engaged in peer editing, this function is not considered useful by teachers. Therefore, for teachers to use technology, they need to develop knowledge that enables them to translate technological potentials into solutions to pedagogical problems, which are very local and deeply situated in their own contexts.

This view of teacher technology knowledge is fairly consistent with findings of cognitive research on teacher knowledge and teacher learning (Putnam & Borko, 2000). A number of cognitive psychologists have argued that human cognition is situated (Greeno, Collins, & Resnick, 1996). According to the *situative* perspective:

> The physical and social contexts in which an activity takes place are an integral part of that activity, and that the activity is an integral part of the learning that takes place within it. How a person learns a particular set of knowledge and skills, and the situation in which a person learns, become a fundamental part of what is learned. Further, whereas traditional cognitive perspectives focus on the individual as the basic unit of analysis, situative perspectives focus on interactive systems that include individuals as participants, interacting with each other as well as materials and representational systems. (Putnam & Borko, 2000, p. 4)

Teachers' knowledge about technology is situated in the context where technology is used. The knowledge is not only about what technology can do but also (and perhaps more importantly) what technology can do for them. The usefulness of a technology lies only in its uses. Thus, teachers' technology knowledge consists of three elements: (a) knowledge of problems that can be solved by technology, (b) knowledge of a technology that can solve their problems, and (c) knowledge of how technology can solve their problems. Teachers who are sufficiently equipped with this knowledge should be able to decide when to use technology and when not to.

They should also be able to select technologies appropriate for the current problems.

This discussion leads us to further questions. First, given the situated nature of teacher technology knowledge and the long list of possible technologies, what technologies should teachers know about? Second, how much should teachers know about specific technologies? Finally, in what ways should teachers learn about technology? I discuss the questions in detail in the following sections.

PENCILS AND MICROSCOPES: WHAT TECHNOLOGIES SHOULD TEACHERS KNOW?

Technology is a very broad and ill-defined term. It can mean any application of human knowledge to practical problems. Even when technology is interpreted as only mechanical objects, the range of objects is almost inexhaustible: from simple things such as the overhead projector and pencil, to complex systems such as the computer and internet. Even when we narrowly define technology as computers, the list of things teachers need to know is still not easy to create.

A useful way to develop such a list might be to first think about the categories of technology teachers may use in their teaching. There are multiple dimensions by which one can group educational technologies: technical capacity, specificity of functions, and pedagogical roles.

In terms of technical capacities, technologies can be grouped into word processing/publishing (e.g., Microsoft Word), data processing (e.g., Access), presentation (e.g., PowerPoint), communication (e.g., e-mail), and information accessing (e.g., web browsers). This way of categorizing currently dominates the discourse in educational technology and teacher education. Many teacher education programs and professional development programs in educational technology are organized around this categorization and teach teachers specific computer applications. Even many state technology requirements for teachers follow this orientation and define teacher technology competency as mastery of applications in these areas (Zhao, Kendall, & Tan, this volume). However, this orientation is too techno-centric, with little consideration of how technology may be used by teachers to solve problems inherent to teaching and learning. In other words, it categorizes technology as artifacts, not tools.

Another way to think about technology is in terms of the types of problems it addresses. Some technologies, such as word processors and web browsers, are content free, multipurpose tools. They can be used in many contexts for a myriad of purposes. In other words, they are like pencils, which can be used for drawing and writing in a variety of situations. On the other hand, some technologies, such as student record management systems or a software program that simulates gravity, are designed for specific purposes. Like microscopes, they are often used in limited situations.

The specificity and versatility of technologies are two opposing qualities. When specificity increases, versatility decreases. Thus, the more specific are the problems a technology is designed to address, the less likely it is that it can be used to address other problems. Specific technologies provide more explicit and constrained connections between functions and problems and thus are easier for teachers to see how they can be used. For example, a student-record management program tells the user clearly what it can do because what it can do is very limited. Consequently, it would be fairly easy for teachers to see how it can be used. However, a more generic technology, such as the word processor, while it allows more creativity, does not suggest any direct connection to an educational problem, making it more difficult for teachers to see how it can be used in their teaching.

The third dimension by which technology can be categorized is its educational function. A number of scholars have proposed categorizations from this perspective. Means (1994) classified educational technology into four categories: used as a tutor, used to explore, applied as a tool, and used to communicate. Technologies used as a tutor are systems designed to "teach by providing information, demonstrations, or simulations in a sequence determined by the system" (p. 11). On the contrary, technologies used to explore are systems that are designed to "facilitate student learning by providing information, demonstrations, or simulations when requested to do so by students" (p. 11). Technologies that are applied as a tool are "general-purpose technological tools for accomplishing such tasks as composition, data storage, or data analysis" (p. 11), while technologies used to communicate are systems that allow "groups of teachers and students to send information and data to each other through networks or other technologies" (p. 11). Bruce and Levin (this volume) propose a similar taxonomy of educational technology. Based on John Dewey's works, they treat technology as media and put educational technologies in four categories as well: technology as media for inquiry, media for construction, media for communication, and media for expression. Salomon (1993) categorized technology into two groups: performance tools and pedagogical tools. Performance tools are technologies that enhance or change how a task is accomplished while pedagogical tools are technologies that focus on changing the user's competencies.

These categorizations of educational technologies are useful for different purposes, but they are not connected to research on teachers' knowledge and beliefs. Without connecting technology to teachers' pedagogies, these categorizations view technology as a separate force in the classroom, while research suggests that the effects of technology are significantly mediated by teachers' existing pedagogical knowledge and beliefs (Becker, 2000; Bruce, 1993; Dwyer, Ringstaff, & Sandholtz, 1991; Fisher, Dwyer, & Yocam, 1996; Zhao, Pugh, Sheldon, & Byers, in press). Thus, what technologies teachers should know should interface directly with what teachers do in their teaching. In other words, teachers' technology knowledge should be integrated with their pedagogical knowledge. Technology knowledge should be considered part of a teacher's knowledge and beliefs about teaching and derived from what he does. Only when such integration is made can technology move from artifact to tool for teachers. And only when technology disappears into teachers' practices (Bruce & Hogan, 1998) and becomes part of their overall knowledge of teaching and learning can technology function to support teaching and learning on a regular basis. Thus, we should consider teachers' technology knowledge in light of their pedagogical knowledge, and consider what technologies teachers should know in light of what they already know and need to know about teaching and learning. The abundant literature on teacher knowledge and teacher learning lends us a conceptual framework for considering teachers' technology knowledge.

There are just as many different categorizations of teacher knowledge and beliefs as categorizations of technology (Borko & Putnam, 1996; Calderhead, 1996; Shulman, 1987). In a review of literature on teacher learning, Borko and Putnam (1996) discussed "three domains of knowledge that are particularly relevant to teachers' instructional practices: (a) general pedagogical knowledge and beliefs, (b) subject matter knowledge and beliefs, and (c) pedagogical content knowledge and beliefs" (p. 675). The two most relevant domains where technology can be applied are general pedagogical knowledge and pedagogical content knowledge. The domain of general pedagogical knowledge and beliefs, according to Borko and Putnam:

> … encompasses a teacher's knowledge and beliefs about teaching, learning, and learners that transcend particular subject matter domains. It includes knowledge of various strategies and arrangements for effective classroom management, instructional strategies for conducting lessons and creating learning environments, and more fundamentally knowledge and beliefs about learners, how they learn, and how that learning can be fostered by teaching. (p. 675)

Pedagogical content knowledge, first proposed by Shulman (1987), includes "the ways of representing and formulating the subject that make it comprehensible to others," and "an understanding of what makes the learning of specific topics easy or difficult" (p. 9).

This articulation of teacher knowledge and beliefs suggests a number of directions for identifying what technologies teachers need to know. First, there is technology for classroom management: databases for record keeping, communication technologies for exchanges with parents, and project management tools for developing and managing class projects. Second, there is technology for instruction: presentation tools to provide multimedia information and simulations, communication tools for students to collaborate on projects, and information accessing technologies for student research. Third, there is technology for teachers to know more about their students: simulation technologies to identify students' misconceptions, technologies for communicating with students, and assessment technologies to better and more accurately gauge student learning. Fourth, there are specific technologies for different subject matters. For example, web-based archives of historical documents can be used for teaching history, live data from the Internet for teaching weather and earthquakes, computer simulations for teaching abstract scientific concepts, writing tools for literacy, and speech technologies for foreign languages.

This articulation of teacher knowledge not only points out that technology knowledge should not be limited to using technology as a tool, but also strongly suggests that teachers understand how technology affects students as well. Today's students grow up in a technology-mediated world and their thinking, behavior, and emotions are heavily influenced by new technologies (Tapscott, 1998). Many students today spend much of their time interacting with technological objects or in technology-mediated environments: watching TV, playing video games, chatting on the Internet, writing on the computer, and reading on the Web. Teachers' knowledge of technology should be expanded to include technologies that students interact with as well.

In summary, instead of treating technology knowledge as a separate entity of teacher knowledge, I suggest that we view it as an integrated part of teacher pedagogical knowledge and pedagogical content knowledge.[1] In other words, technology becomes an element of instructional and classroom management strategies. Knowledge of teaching, learning, and content includes knowledge of technology.

FROM ADOPTION TO INVENTION: HOW MUCH SHOULD TEACHERS KNOW ABOUT TECHNOLOGY?

There are two dimensions of knowledge: breadth and depth. Breadth indicates the quantity of technologies teachers need to know while depth refers to how much teachers need to know about each technology. Thus far, I have discussed the breadth of technology knowledge. In this section I discuss the issue of depth of technology teachers should develop.

Teachers' technology knowledge can have three levels: mechanical, meaningful, and generative. At a *mechanical* level, users' understanding of a technology is fragmented, limited, and superficial, focusing more on form than function. Teachers who are at this level of proficiency hold relatively stereotypical views of the functions of the technology—similar to what is conceived in popular media or by the manufacturer. Typical behaviors of teachers who understand technology at a mechanical level include following strictly prescribed steps of action when approaching technology, attempting to memorize specific instructions for how to use a particular technology, and an inability or reluctance to use new and unfamiliar technologies.

At the *meaningful* level, users begin to separate functions from forms. They can think of or accept alternative ways to achieve the same function. Though they begin to gain a certain situational awareness about technology, they are still limited in their ability to use or repurpose the tools in new or different contexts. At the *generative* level of technology proficiency, users have a deep understanding of the technology, which enables them to disassociate form from function and break away from stereotypical uses of technology. These users also have a good understanding of the contextual implications of the technology and are sensitive to appropriate and inappropriate uses of technological tools.

The depth of teacher technology knowledge significantly affects their uses of technology (Zhao et al., in press). Teachers at the mechanical level of understanding often try to repeat what technical manuals prescribe or what they are taught. They are less inclined to repurpose technology for their own uses. On the other hand, teachers at the generative level of knowledge are creative and frequently reinterpret technology for their purposes. They adapt technology instead of adopting it.

The Apple Classroom of Tomorrow (ACOT) project (Fisher et al., 1996), one of the first and most extensive large-scale experiments with infusing technology in all aspects of teaching found that teachers go through a five-stage evolution in their uses of technology: entry, adoption, adaptation, appropriation, and invention (Sandholtz & Ringstaff, 1996; Sandholtz, Ringstaff, & Dwyer, 1997). In the entry stage, teachers did not have much experience with technology—it could be said that their technology knowledge was at a mechanical level. Their focus was on changes in the physical environment and on "typical first-year-teacher problems such as discipline, resource management, and personal frustrations" (Sandholtz & Ringstaff, 1996, p. 286). Their use of technological resources was simple and limited.

In the adoption stage, teachers began to develop more fluency with technology. They became more focused on the functions of technology. "Their concerns shifted from connecting the computers to using them" (Sandholtz

& Ringstaff, 1996, p. 286). When they moved into the adaptation stage, "teachers increasingly incorporated technology in their instruction" (p. 286). They began to observe improved efficiency of the instructional process and notice changes in student learning and engagement.

The last two stages, appropriation and invention, saw more creative uses of technology to accomplish real tasks. Teachers at these stages should have reached the generative level in terms of technology knowledge.

> They came to understand technology and used it effortlessly to accomplish real work—their roles began to shift noticeably and new instructional patterns emerged ... teachers began to reflect on teaching, to question old patterns, to speculate about causes behind the changes they were seeing in their students. (Sandholtz & Ringstaff, 1996, p. 287)

This indicates freedom from technology. Teachers are no longer constrained by the prescribed mechanical functions of technology. They invent and reinvent the uses of technology in their own teaching. In these last stages, technology has become part of teacher knowledge and pedagogy.

In summary, how much teachers know about technology makes a big difference in their uses of technology, as suggested by the ACOT study (Fisher et al., 1996). Once technology is truly integrated, teachers' beliefs and knowledge are changed as well. New pedagogical knowledge and practices emerge from the integration of technology, but only when teachers reach a certain level of technology understanding. Thus, when considering what teachers should know about technology, we cannot only think about what and how many technologies but also how much.

FROM ADDITION TO INTEGRATION: HOW TO TEACH TEACHERS TECHNOLOGY?

As teacher education programs are asked to prepare technologically proficient teachers, they are faced with the practical problem of how to teach teachers to use technology. The first and usual response is to offer a new course, as we have always done when something new needs to be taught. Actually many teacher education programs have been offering educational technology courses for a long time, although their content has changed many times. Lumsdaine (1963) reported that in some states, teachers were required to take a lab course to learn how to use films for teaching in the 1960s. As technologies changed over the years, the emphasis in lab courses moved from films to instructional television, personal computers, multimedia authoring, and the Internet.

Adding a new course on technology to an existing program has a number of benefits. First, it ensures that the content, whatever it is and whoever defines it, has a place in the curriculum. Someone is responsible for this part of teacher knowledge. Second, it is fairly easy to implement. A program needs only to find one or two instructors and hand them this job. It does not affect the rest of the faculty, thus causing minimal disruption to existing practices. Finally, it is more noticeable to the accreditation agency and the public that the program has addressed the issue of preparing teachers to use technology.

This addition approach, however, is quite problematic in at least two ways. First, today's school technology is rather different from its predecessors such as films and overhead projectors. Computer-based technologies are much more complex than older technologies and encompass a wider range of applications. One course is no longer sufficient to help teachers reach the level of knowledge needed for creative use. Adding more courses is at the same time next to impossible because most teacher programs already have a crowded curriculum. Second, and more important, as discussed earlier in this essay, technology should be considered part of teachers' pedagogical knowledge. Teaching technology separately could easily result in a focus on technological skills instead of technology uses.

An alternative approach that is gaining popularity is to integrate technology into the existing courses. Instead of offering separate technology courses, some teacher education programs have started to infuse technology into the current curriculum. Every teacher education course becomes a place where future teachers can learn how to use technology. The integration approach should theoretically be more effective than the addition approach. It enables teacher educators to demonstrate how technology can be used in authentic teaching situations, and provides opportunities for pre-service teachers to explore and use technology throughout their collegiate years. It provides possibilities for connecting technology to content knowledge, pedagogical knowledge, and pedagogical content knowledge, which is the main focus of most teacher education courses. For this reason, the integration approach is more likely to teach technology uses rather than technical skills.

However, the integration approach is much more challenging to implement than the addition approach because it requires instructors of all teacher education courses to be able to use technology to teach, and understand how technology can be used for classroom management and instruction. This is no easy task however, as many teacher educators are no better prepared to use technology than are K–12 teachers (The CEO Forum on Education and Technology, 1999). Taking the integration approach requires teacher education programs to invest much more in professional development for their teaching staff and to provide sufficient technical support as well as access to facilities. Further, integration could mean disappearance—the technology component can be easily ignored or taken out by instructors who are not prepared to teach with technology or are pressured for time to teach "more important" things for teachers. The effectiveness of the integration approach relies heavily on the readiness of the teacher education faculty.

CONCLUSION

What I have done so far is to unpack the question "what should teachers know about technology?" To reach a useful answer to this question, we need to address at least four more questions: What is the nature of technology use? What technologies should teachers know? How much should teachers know about technology? Finally, how can teacher education programs teach technology knowledge? These four questions constitute the main components of a framework for future inquiries about teacher technology knowledge.

I have attempted to propose some tentative answers to these questions:

1. Technology use is essentially a process whereby the user turns an artifact into a tool, an object into a solution to a local problem.
2. Technology should be considered an integral part of teacher knowledge. Teacher pedagogical knowledge and beliefs should include knowledge of how technology can be used to solve their own problems. Therefore, a good source of directions for identifying what technologies teachers should know is what they already do and know.
3. Teachers can have different levels of technology understandings. The levels of understanding matter in teaching practices.
4. Teacher education programs could take two different approaches to teach technology: separate technology courses or integration of technology into the existing curriculum. Each approach has its merits and problems.

These answers are summaries of current understandings and are meant to serve as a starting point for future research. Many of the ideas discussed in this essay are speculative in nature and await further verification. The papers included in this volume address these issues in more detail through a variety of perspectives and methods.

NOTE

1. There are different ways to conceptualize teacher technology knowledge in relation to pedagogical knowledge. In other chapters of this volume, the authors hold different perspectives on what teacher technology knowledge is, for example, see Margerum-Leys and Marx (this volume) and Conway and Zhao (this volume).

REFERENCES

Aesop. (1912). *Aesop's fables* (S. Vernon Jones, Trans.). New York: Avenel Books.

Becker, H.J. (1999). *Internet use by teachers*. Irvine, CA: Center for Research on Information Technology and Organizations (CRITO), University of California at Irvine.

Becker, H.J. (2000). Findings from the teaching, learning, and computing survey: Is Larry Cuban right? *Education Policy Analysis Archives, 8*(51), 2–32.

Borko, H., & Putnam, R.T. (1996). Learning to teach. In D.C. Berliner & R.C. Calfee (Eds.), *Handbook of educational psychology* (pp. 673–708). New York: Macmillan.

Bromley, H. (1998). Introduction: Data-driven democracy? Social assessment of educational computing. In H. Bromley & M. Apple (Eds.), *Education, technology, power* (pp. 1–28). Albany: SUNY Press.

Bruce, B.C. (1993). Innovation and social change. In B.C. Bruce, J.K. Peyton, & T. Batson (Eds.), *Network-based classrooms* (pp. 32). Cambridge: Cambridge University Press.

Bruce, B.C., & Hogan, M.P. (1998). The disappearance of technology: Toward an ecological model of literacy. In D. Reinking, M.C. McKenna, L.D. Labbo, & R.D. Kieffer (Eds.), *Handbook of Literacy and technology: Transformations in a post-typographic world* (p. 281). Mahwah, NJ: Erlbaum.

Calderhead, J. (1996). Teachers: Beliefs and knowledge. In D.C. Berliner & R.C. Calfee (Eds.), *Handbook of educational psychology* (pp. 709–725). New York: Macmillan.

Cattagni, A., & Farris, E. (2001). *Internet access in U.S. public schools and classrooms: 1994–2000*. Washington, DC: National Center for Educational Statistics.

CEO Forum on Education and Technology. (1999). *School technology and readiness report: Year 2*. Washington, DC: The CEO Forum on Education and Technology.

Cuban, L. (1986). *Teachers and machines: The classroom uses of technology since 1920*. New York: Teachers College Press.

Cuban, L. (1999, August 4). The technology puzzle: Why is greater access not translating into better classroom use? *Education Week*, pp. 68, 47.

Cuban, L. (2001). *Oversold and underused: Computers in schools 1980–2000*. Cambridge, MA: Harvard University Press.

Dwyer, D.C., Ringstaff, C., & Sandholtz, J. (1991, May). Change in teachers' beliefs and practices in technology-rich classrooms. *Educational Leadership*, pp. 45–52.

Edelfelt, R.A., & Raths, J.D. (1999). *A brief history of standards in teacher education*. Reston, VA: Association of Teacher Educators.

Fisher, C., Dwyer, D.C., & Yocam, K. (Eds.). (1996). *Education and technology: Reflections on computing in classrooms.* San Francisco: Jossey-Bass.

Gage, N.L. (1963). *Handbook of research on teaching.* Chicago: Rand McNally & Company.

Greeno, J.G., Collins, A.M., & Resnick, L.B. (1996). Cognition and learning. In D. Berliner & R. Calfee (Eds.), *Handbook of educational psychology* (pp. 15–46). New York: Macmillan.

Hickman, L.A. (1990). *John Dewey's pragmatic technology.* Bloomington: Indiana University Press.

Loveless, T. (1996). Why aren't computers used more in schools? *Educational Policy, 10*(4), 448–467.

Lumsdaine, A.A. (1963). Instruments and media of instruction. In N.L. Gage (Ed.), *Handbook of research on teaching* (pp. 683–714). Chicago: Rand McNally & Company.

Means, B. (1994). Introduction: Using technology to advance educational goals. In B. Means (Ed.), *Technology and education reform* (pp. 1–21). San Francisco: Jossey-Bass.

National Council for Accreditation of Teacher Education. (1997). *Technology and the new professional teacher: Preparing for the 21st century classroom.* Washington, DC: Author.

Putnam, R. T., & Borko, H. (2000). What do new views of knowledge and thinking have to say about research on teacher learning? *Educational Researcher, 29*(1), 4–15.

Richardson, V. (Ed.). (2001). *Handbook of research on teaching* (4th ed.). Washington, DC: American Educational Research Association.

Salomon, G. (1993). On the nature of pedagogic computer tools: The case of the writing partner. In S.P. Lajoie & S.J. Derry (Eds.), *Computers as cognitive tools* (pp. 179–196). Hillsdale, NJ: Erlbaum.

Sandholtz, J.H., & Ringstaff, C. (1996). Teacher change in technology-rich classrooms. In C. Fisher, D.C. Dwyer, & K. Yocam (Eds.), *Education and technology: Reflections on computing in classrooms* (pp. 281–299). San Francisco: Jossey-Bass.

Sandholtz, J.H., Ringstaff, C., & Dwyer, D.C. (1997). *Teaching with technology: Creating student-centered classrooms.* New York: Teachers College Press.

Shulman, L.S. (1987). Knowledge and teaching: Foundations of the new reform. *Harvard Education Review, 57*(1), 1–22.

Smerdon, B., Cronen, S., Lanahan, L., Anderson, J., Iannotti, N., & Angeles, J. (2000). *Teachers' tools for the 21st century: A report on teachers' use of technology.* Washington, DC: National Center for Educational Statistics.

Tapscott, D. (1998). *Growing up digital: The rise of the net generation.* New York: McGraw-Hill.

Travers, R.M.W. (1973). *Second handbook of research on teaching.* Chicago: Rand McNally & Company.

U.S. Congress, Office of Technology Assessment. (1995). *Teachers and technology: Making the connection* (OTA-EHR-616). Washington, DC: Office of Technology Assessment.

Wittrock, M.C. (Ed.). (1986). *Handbook of research on teaching* (3rd ed.). New York: Macmillan.

Zhao, Y., Pugh, K., Sheldon, S., & Byers, J. (in press). Conditions for classroom technology innovations. *Teachers College Record.*

CHAPTER 2

FROM LUDDITES TO DESIGNERS

Portraits of Teachers and Technology in Political Documents

Paul Conway and Yong Zhao

INTRODUCTION

Portraits of the relationship between teachers and machines have changed in the various waves of educational technology in U.S. schools over the last 100 years. Nowhere is this more obvious than in the recent proliferation of educational technology plans in response to the information and communication technologies (ICTs) revolution (Naughton, 1999). A number of national reports have done a very good job conveying the message that technology holds great potential for education, but students are not using it to improve their learning because (a) they do not have access to adequate hardware and software and (b) their teachers have not been adequately prepared. This message is fueling the multibillion dollar frenzy to get technology into schools and provide technology training to teachers. Accompanying this campaign for technology in schools is the dramatic

What Should Teachers Know About Technology?: Perspectives and Practices, pages 15–30
Copyright © 2003 by Information Age Publishing
All rights of reproduction in any form reserved.

growth in technology plans. These plans serve as frameworks for integrating technology in education at the state, district, and school level. As an important rhetorical device used by state and local educational policy makers, who are behind the generous spending on technology, these plans also attempt to convince the public that technology ought to be integrated into education as an effective solution to a myriad of educational problems. In this paper, our primary concern is the portrayal of teachers in state educational technology plans. However, we first set the context for our discussion, of the portrayal of teachers, by addressing the political context out of which educational technology plans emerged and address their discourse shaping power.

The National Educational Technology plan, released in 2000 by the U.S. Department of Education, is a telling example. Educational technology plans are not only a rhetorical device or political exercise. They have serious financial and technological consequences, which in turn have great implications for educational practices, such as teacher professional development. Technology plans are quite often a prerequisite for accessing major funding opportunities, such as the five year, two billion dollar Technology Challenge Funds, and the more than five billion dollar Universal Service Fund (e-Rate), which means schools and state educational agencies must develop technology plans in order to obtain technology funding. In other words, schools that do not have an acceptable technology plan are not eligible to apply for the Technology Challenge Funds or the Universal Service Fund. Furthermore, the state technology plan is used to guide technology spending in the state. For instance, the State of Michigan has consistently followed the recommendations in its state technology plan in dispensing around 60 million dollars from the Technology Literacy Challenge Fund over the past four years. The Michigan State Technology plan was used as the basis for identifying funding priorities. Moreover, portions of the funds were set aside for projects that specifically address the recommendations of the technology plan. More than five million dollars have been allocated to these statewide projects, each of which was required to identify one or more recommendations in Michigan's Technology Plan as a focal point of their efforts. Additionally, even projects proposed by local schools must be consistent with recommendations of the State Technology plan, as the 1999 Request for Proposals from Michigan Department of Education clearly stipulates.

In the remainder of the paper, we first present a brief description of the nature of state technology plans. We then describe how we selected, coded, and analyzed fifteen state technology plans in terms of their portrayal of teachers. We then present our findings. We conclude this paper with a discussion of two issues. First, we address the significance of the portrayal of teachers in the technology plans in light of research findings about educational reform. Second, we expand on our conception of teachers as designers and its power as an image of teachers in terms of the pedagogical ecology of classrooms. In doing so, we address the ways in which the portrayal of teachers as designers reconfigures the relationship between teachers, technology, and knowledge.

WHAT ARE STATE TECHNOLOGY PLANS?

State technology plans are state level policy documents that provide frameworks for implementing educational technology in the state. These plans were usually constructed by a committee composed of educational stakeholders. A typical committee consisted of representatives of the state department of education, private businesses, district administrators, school board members, university faculty, K–12 teachers, district technology specialists, and various professional organizations. Most plans were then sent to the state board of education for approval. Upon approval, they became legal documents that would guide state spending on educational technology.

POSSIBLE VIEWS OF TEACHERS IN THE CONTEXT OF TECHNOLOGY: TEACHERS AND MACHINES IN THE LAST 100 YEARS

The portrayal of teachers in relation to technology has changed considerably over the last century in response to the various waves of technological innovation (e.g., radio in the 1930s, overhead projector in the 1940s, television in the 1950s and 1960s, microcomputer in the 1980s, information and communication technologies in the 1990s and beyond). Changes in the ways teachers have been portrayed reflect reconfigurations of the relationships envisaged between knowledge, teachers, and technology. In reviewing the literature on teachers and technology, three views are apparent over time: teachers as Luddites, as gatekeepers, and as designers.

Teachers as Luddites

Luddites, a term coined after Ned Ludd, an 18th century English laborer who was supposed to have destroyed weaving machinery in the belief that such machinery would diminish employment, is often used to refer to those who opposed technical or technological change. Thus, the image of teachers as Luddites, who for fear of being replaced by technology actively resist the introduction of technology, fit very well with traditional images of the teacher as the preeminent source of information. Portrayals of technology-laden, teacher-free classrooms brought about by the information dispensing efficiency of radio, television, or computer-assisted instruction (CAI) characterize this view. In this scenario, teachers and technology were natural adversaries with teachers also doomed to lose the information transmission competition because information technology was considered to be a more reliable source of more updated information than teachers. It was also believed that information technology could more economically and effectively transmit the information.

Teachers as Gatekeepers

Early hopes about how efficient innovative technologies would replace the teacher were dashed, however, by a realization that teachers actually decide what technologies may enter the classroom and whether and how they could be used (Cuban, 1986; Noble, 1996). Research in technology adoption, thus, suggests a different view of the teacher—teacher as gatekeeper. According to this view, teachers decide whether, what, and how technology gets used in classrooms (Cuban, 1986; Office of Technology Assessment, 1995). In addition, research in cognitive psychology has supported this notion that teachers were active decision-makers (Clark & Peterson, 1986; Morine-Dershimer & Corrigan, 1997; Shavelson, 1976). This view of the teacher as decision-maker or filter heralded an appreciative but also exasperated view of the role of teachers in relationship to technology. On the one hand, there was an appreciation of how teachers were important interpreters of the way technology ought to be used in classrooms to promote student learning (Bruce, 1993). However, on the other hand, there was exasperation at how teachers often foiled the best-laid plans of how technology could improve student learning because of the teachers' inability or unwillingness to use technology in their classrooms (Cuban, 1986).

Teachers as Designers

A more recent view of teachers in relationship to technology sees teachers as designers. In this view, teachers, rather than taking on the role of knowledge dispensers or just adopting existing technologies, design their own teaching environment with a variety of technological tools to facilitate knowledge construction. Moreover, teachers, like an architect, actively engage themselves in exploring the possibilities and constraints of technologies and other materials to construct the best environment to fulfill their pedagogical expectations. Technology is no longer considered a cure-all tool, but rather a component of the pedagogical ecology. From this perspective teachers are not only adopters or implementers of technology, but also developers, evaluators, and designers.

SELECTION OF STATE TECHNOLOGY PLANS

Having become generally familiar with the format and contents of the state technology plans nationally, we selected fifteen state technology plans for further analysis. These plans were selected for their representativeness according to state population size (Texas to New Jersey), geographical dispersion (from Alaska to Maryland), and time of creation (1993 to 1997). We accessed the plans at their respective web sites. Table 2.1 lists the states whose technology plans were selected and analyzed in the study.

Analysis

We developed categories (Luddites, gatekeepers, and designers) as a result of our analysis of the technology plans, a review of relevant literature, and our knowledge of the views of teachers in relation to technology, in previous and current waves of technological innovation in education. We then individually coded the portrayal of teachers in each state plan based on these categories. Subsequently, we cross-checked our results in an iterative fashion to ensure adequate reliability. When there was any disagreement, we discussed our different interpretations to reach a consensus. Table 2.2 presents the categories we developed.

Views of Teachers in Technology Plans

Technology will never replace teachers. Technology may, though, serve a pivotal role in displacing ineffective, unwilling teachers. When coupled with appropriate peripheral equipment and excellent software, technology will assist teachers in many ways that are not imagined currently. All Mississippi educators must stay alert, though, to ensure that teaching is conducted properly. (Mississippi Department of Education, 1996, ch. 8.1)

The above excerpt from the Mississippi plan exemplifies a stance shared by many state technology plans. Teachers are portrayed as gatekeepers or adopters across all states rather than as Luddites or designers (see Table 2.2).

Table 2.1. State Technology Summaries

State	www Site	Technology Literacy Challenge Fund	Other federal funds	Number of students	Students to multi-media computer ratio	Number of teachers	Technology trained teachers
Alaska	www.educ.state.ak.us/	FY 1997: $1 mil. FY 1998: $2.1 mil.	$1.2 mil.	126,015	16:1	7,644	21%
Colorado	www.cde.state.co.us	FY 1997: $1.9 mil. FY 1998: $3.9 mil.	$1.4 mil.	673,438	20:1	35,900	20%
Connecticut	www.state.ct.us/sde/dsi/technology/csetp.pdf	FY 1997: $1.5 mil. FY 1998: $3.8 mil.	$1.2 mil.	523,054	22:1	36,800	15%
Georgia	www.doe.k12.ga.us	FY 1997: $4.8 mil. FY 1998: $10.9 mil.	$712,048	1,321,239	18:1	81,683	18%
Illinois	www.isbe.state.il.us/homepage.html	FY 1997: $9.1 mil. FY 1998: $17.9 mil.	$3.7 mil.	1,961,299	20:1	115,859	10%
Indiana	www.doe.state.in.us	FY 1997: $3.1 mil. FY 1998: $6.2 mil.	$1.8 mil.	984,610	19:1	56,412	13%
Kansas	www.ksbe.state.ks.us/pubs/techguide.html	FY 1997: $1.5 mil. FY 1998: $3 mil.	$526,699 + $883,359	465,140	11:1	30,750	15%
Kentucky	www.kde.state.ky.us/	FY 1997: $3.5 mil. FY 1998: $6.9 mil.	$2.4 mil.	663,071	23:1	39,235	28%

Table 2.1. State Technology Summaries (Cont.)

State	www Site	Technology Literacy Challenge Fund	Other federal funds	Number of students	Students to multi-media computer ratio	Number of teachers	Technology trained teachers
Maryland	www.sailor.lib.md.us/msde/	FY 1997: $2.4 mil. FY 1998: $5.5 mil.	$1.8 mil.	818,947	23:1	47,005	15%
Michigan	www.mde.state.mi.us/	FY 1997: $8.6 mil. FY 1998: $18.2 mil.	$2.5 mil.	1,662,100	20:1	84,200	10%
Mississippi	www.mdek12.state.ms.us/	FY 1997: $3.5 mil. FY 1998: $6.7 mil.	$1.5 mil.	504,168	28:1	29,237	11%
Nebraska	http://nde4.nde.state.ne.us/	FY 1997: $1 mil. FY 1998: $2.1 mil.	$4.3 mil.	292,121	13:1	20,109	15%
New Mexico	www.education.lanl.gov/resources/oii/nmplan/stateplan.html	FY 1997: $1.7 mil. FY 1998: $3.5 mil.	$1.2 mil.	330,522	23:1	19,608	10%
Texas	www.tea.state.tx.us/	FY 1997: $16.3 mil. FY 1998: $35.3 mil.	$2.8 mil.	3,809,186	20:1	247,526	18%
Vermont	www.state.vt.us/educ/	FY 1997: $1 mil. FY 1998: $2.1 mil.	$145,633 + $533,383	106,607	25:1	7,787	18%

Source: Education Week (1997). Available at http://www.edweek.org/sreports/tc/policy/states/usmap.htm

Table 2.2.   Images of Teachers in State Technology Plans

State	Luddite	Gatekeeper or filter	Designers
Alaska		Y	
Connecticut		Y	
Colorado		Y	
Georgia		Y	
Illinois		Y	Y
Indiana		Y	
Kansas		Y	
Kentucky		Y	
Maryland		Y	
Michigan		Y	
Mississippi	Y	Y	
Nebraska		Y	
New Mexico		Y	
Texas	Y	Y	
Vermont		Y	
Total %	13.33	100	6.66

Luddite = teachers viewed as completely resistant to technology
Gatekeeper or filter = teachers viewed as central decision-makers in technology
adoption and usage. As primary filters they need to be trained to use technology
Designers = teachers viewed as creative and imaginative designers of technology usage in school settings

This conclusion, while it may seem a rather banal observation, is important to note in the context of previous waves of technological innovation in education, which have sought to replace teachers. The view of teachers in the plans was more positive than the image of teacher as intractable Luddite. Images of teacher as convertible Luddite but primarily as gatekeeper were evident in the technology plans (see Table 2.2). A few plans, for example, anticipated that a minority of teachers might be resistant to technology. Common across the three views of teachers in the technology plans is the sense that teachers, whatever attitude they hold toward technology, need training in technology. As stated in the Georgia plan:

Educators must simultaneously be challenged and supported in order to develop expertise with new technological innovations and to implement the new learning in their classrooms. (Georgia State Department of Education, 1997, p. 39)

Providing training to teachers serves different functions depending on the view one holds of teachers. For those who believe teachers are convertible Luddites, the training is expected to convince teachers that technology will assist them rather than replace them, that computers are "allies," not "aliens." For those who view teachers as gatekeepers, the training is expected to convince the teachers to open their doors to technology and teach them appropriate ways of technology integration. Most technology plans seem to stop here in terms of training and professional development. Except for the K–12 Information Technology Plan for the State of Illinois, we did not find any plan that viewed teachers as designers, for whom the training should provide opportunities and resources for exploration, construction, and design.

This view of teachers as workers in need of training was sometimes based on a deficit model of teacher knowledge. Nevertheless, teachers were viewed as central players and gatekeepers in technology adoption. The Texas technology plan emphatically stated that:

> To provide quality education to all learners, the training and retooling of the current educator workforce in using technology tools to teach and learn must be identified as a priority. (Texas Education Agency, 1996, p. 31)

However, professional development is not descriptive enough of what is entailed for teachers:

> This staff development is not merely short term. Instead it is a re-tooling of a statewide workforce of more than 250,000 professionals. (Texas Education Agency, 1996, p. 18)

"Retooling" projects an outright jettisoning of older tools and full-scale introduction of new tools. Conspicuously absent from this vision of teachers in need of retooling is an appreciation and acknowledgment of teachers' knowledge of various existing technologies and their relationship to student learning and classroom processes.

Driven by the belief that knowledge about technology and its potential educational benefits would help convert the Luddites or loosen up the gatekeepers, the state technology plans consistently stipulate that teachers must meet certain technology competency requirements. Underlying this stipulation was often a decontextualized notion of learning whereby teachers would learn and then apply technology in their teaching. The Texas technology plan tried to hedge its bets in this regard, at one point stating that teachers need to *first* learn technology: "teachers must first be competent with the technology applications that facilitate their work and support student learning" (Texas Education Agency, 1996, p. 23). This approach implies delivery of skills prior to and separate from context of usage. However, later the document states that teacher professional development will adopt a just-in-time rather than a just-in-case model. Just-in-time professional development "rejects the standard of often irrelevant or ill-timed professional development presented just in case one ever needs it" (Texas Education Agency, 1996, p. 32).

Summary

Thus far, we have presented our findings of the portrayal of teachers evident in 15 state technology plans. We presented these views in light of a wide range of possible views derived from the literature on educational technology to point out what views are missing. We use this section to summarize our main findings and address the implications of our major observations of the state educational technology plans portrayal of teachers.

To summarize, we have come to the following conclusions based on our analysis of the portrayal of teachers in state technology plans. First, in terms of teachers, our reading of the technology plans suggests that the plans do acknowledge that teachers are important in technology adoption but do not go as far as to identify ways in which teachers can be resourceful, knowledgeable, and purposeful designers of educational technology. Second, a common feature of all state educational technology plans was the skillful use of sales techniques which capitalize on our fear of being left behind, hope for quick and simple solutions to complex teacher professional development challenges, and a dream of a utopian future. The utopian images of technologies' potential are in contrast to the more cautious portrayal of teachers. The following excerpts from Texas' educational technology plan (Texas Education Agency, 1996) epitomize such techniques:

Imagine a home…

… where every parent regardless of native language or socioeconomic background can communicate readily with teachers about children's progress, improve parenting skills, and get a degree or job training without leaving home or work.

Imagine a school…

… where every student regardless of zip code, economic level, age, race or ethnicity, or ability or disability can be immersed in the sights, sounds, and languages of other countries; visit museums; research knowledge webs from the holdings of dispersed libraries; and explore the inner workings of cells from inside the cell or the cold distance of outer space from inside a virtual spacesuit.

Who, in their right mind, would refuse to work for such a wonderful future! The seductive image painted in the above excerpts sets in motion a sales pitch, typical of the other state educational technology plans we reviewed. In sum, state technology plans privileged an innovative over a social practice discourse (Bruce, 1993). This privileging of an innovative discourse was nowhere more apparent than in the conception of positive, ceaseless, inevitable educational change as a consequence of adopting the new technologies. It is no surprise for the state technology plans to take the form of idealistic vision statements because such statements are needed to rally political support. However, in terms of the portrayal of teachers, the pattern of privileging innovative over social practice discourse in state technology plans is problematic for a number of reasons:

- It presents, what we see, as a constricted portrayal of teachers' role in relationship to technology. Teachers are seen as responsive to technology in various ways rather than as creators and designers of technology-rich learning environments. Consequently, the potential roles teachers might play in professional development initiatives in relation to technology are constrained;
- It underestimates the complexity of social change inherent in educational reform by overselling technology as *the solution* or *deus ex machina* for education (Cohen, 1988; Fullan, 1991; Sarason, 1993). Consequently, it constricts the portrayal of teachers' possible roles in relation to technology; and
- It is guilty of technocentrism that both dupes us into believing in technologically-driven progress and eliminates a conversation about the possibilities and constraints of computer hardware generally, and specifically about the variety of software packages available, each with its own constellation of possibilities and problems.

Consequently, the cumulative effect of this discourse pattern, is that it scotomizes (Sacks, 1995) teachers' potential role as designers (Zhao, 1998). In the next section of this paper, we expand on what we mean by teachers as designers and discuss the implications of this view for teachers' professional development.

DISCUSSION

Who are the designers in today's world? Landscape and fashion designers, songwriters and software designers, architects and artists, potters and playwrights come to mind, to name but a few. Each of these designers has a purpose and engages in their design work in a particular context. For the playwright, the purposes may be to entertain and enthrall, and the context may be imagining the enactment of the word, of the text. What are the common features of design-type roles? Typically, design-type roles demand not merely the application of knowledge to known contexts, rather they involve problem framing and solving, nuanced interpretation, uncertainty, and the drawing together of resources and tools in a particular context to create a new configuration of ideas, images, or artifacts. In many respects, we see design is akin to what Schön (1983) calls a "reflective conversation with the situation" (pp. 241–2). In portraying teachers as designers, we ask two questions: For what purpose(s) can we view teachers as designers? In what contexts are teachers designing?

Teachers as Designers: For What Purpose(s)?

For most of the last 100 years, the goals of the education system were focused on educating a minority with high levels of skill and knowledge, and educating the rest with basic literacy, numeracy, and civic values. Today, the goals have shifted radically. No longer is it sufficient to only educate a few to frame and solve problems, engage in vigorous debate, deal with uncertainty, and regulate their own learning. Rather, these vital outcomes are now needed and being seen as essential for *all* in a rapidly changing knowledge-based society (National Research Council, 2000). All learners must now meet more ambitious educational goals involving higher-order thinking (Resnick, 1987). In this scenario, it makes little sense to expect teachers to educate problem solvers and self-regulating lifelong learners, if their own professional development roles do not nurture and extend their potential role as designers of technology-rich learning environments. In conceptualizing the education of teachers as designers in the context of technological innovation, we inevitably have to ask what are teachers actually designing.

Teachers as Designers: Designing What Contexts?

The advent of numerous information and communication technologies has brought about the possibility of making significant changes in the pedagogical ecology of classrooms and schools congruent with advances in the learning sciences (National Research Council, 2000). For teachers, the emergence of these new technologies, in our view, presents a powerful but challenging invitation to redesign classrooms, moving from transmission-oriented modes of instruction to more constructivist-compatible pedagogy. The challenge, we think for teachers, is to design technology-rich learning environments, based on what the Cognition and Technology Group at

Vanderbilt (CTGV, 1996) view as the two waves of the cognitive revolution. The first wave drew our attention to actively engaging the individual thinker and learner, and doing so with little or no attention to emotions, context, culture, and history (Gardner, 1985). The second wave is attempting to reintegrate cognition within its social, cultural, and historical contexts (Brown, Ash, Rutherford, Nakagawa, Gordon, & Campione, 1993; CTGV, 1996). In this vein, Roschelle, Pea, Hoadley, Gordon, and Means (2000), in their recent study of what and how schools can be changed with computer-based technologies, identified four characteristics of learning that can be supported in technology rich environments. These conditions are (a) active engagement by learners, (b) participation in groups, (c) frequent interaction and feedback, and (d) connections to real world contexts. However, they emphasize that the potential of technology to tap into these learning characteristics is not automatic. Rather, they note that: "...the use of technology as an effective learning tool is more likely to take place when embedded in a larger educational reform movement" (p. 76). In this context, it becomes crucial to ally teachers' knowledge about not only various general pedagogical approaches, but also pedagogical content knowledge, as well as the learning affordances and constraints of various computer-based technologies allied with the current more ambitious reform-based educational goals for students. We now turn to what teachers need to know in order to design in technology rich environments.

Toward a New Vision of What Teachers Need to Know

Shulman's (1987) framework for conceptualizing teacher knowledge incorporates (a) general pedagogical knowledge and beliefs, (b) subject matter knowledge and beliefs, and (c) pedagogical content knowledge and beliefs. We think, given the proliferation of information and communication technologies and their myriad uses to meet learning goals, that it is no longer sufficient to include "technology" as part of general pedagogical knowledge and beliefs. Rather, we think it would be helpful to think of, what we call, pedagogical content technology knowledge and beliefs, as another category of teacher knowledge. We see technology knowledge as more akin to pedagogical content knowledge, which is subject-specific knowledge, rather than general pedagogical knowledge, since the affordances and constraints of various technologies are best understood within the context of subject matter teaching. Dewey's distinction between the logical and psychological aspects of experience is helpful here in shifting the focus to learning in the context of technology.

Dewey, in *The Child and the Curriculum* (1902/1956), distinguishes between the logical and the psychological aspects of experience. The former he claimed "standing for the subject matter itself, the latter for it in relation to the child" (p. 283). Thus, we might surmise that, from Dewey's distinction between the logical and psychological aspects of curriculum content, teachers in teaching *about* technology and teaching *with* technology are responsible for the psychologizing of technology. That is, "turned over, translated into the immediate and individual experiencing within which it has its origins and significance" (p. 285). According the Shulman and Quinlan (1996) the psychologizing of subject matter has two interacting aspects:

> It reconnects the subject matter to the psychological processes of discovery and deliberation pursued by the mature scholars. It also involves the transformation of its mature and crystallized forms into representations that will be meaningful and educative to the child. The psychologized subject matter is faithful to both of its constituents—the child and the curriculum. (p. 402)

In conclusion, state technology plans portray teachers as gatekeepers. We made a case for thinking of teachers as designers as well as outlining our conception of design. To some extent, both of these images are consistent with current thinking about teacher professional development. However, limiting the role of teachers to the latter portrays a rather limited role for the teacher.

REFERENCES

Brown, A.L., Ash, D., Rutherford, M., Nakagawa, K., Gordon, A., & Campione, J. (1993). Distributed expertise in the classroom. In G. Salomon (Ed.), *Distributed cognitions: Psychological and educational considerations.* New York: Cambridge University Press.

Bruce, B.C. (1993). Innovation and social change. In B.C. Bertram, J. Peyton, & T. Batson. (Eds.) *Network-based classrooms: Promises and realities.* New York: Cambridge University Press.

Clark, C.M., & Peterson, P.L. (1986). Teachers' thought processes. In M.C. Wittrock (Ed.) *Handbook of research on teaching* (3rd ed.). New York: Macmillan.

Cohen, D.K. (1988). Teaching practice: Plus change. In P.W. Jackson (Ed.), *Contributing to educational change: Perspectives on research and practice* (pp. 27–84). Berkeley, CA: McCutchan.

Cognition and Technology and Group at Vanderbilt (CTGV). (1996). A framework for understanding technology and education research. In D.C. Berliner & R. Calfee (Ed.), *Handbook of educational psychology.* New York: Macmillan.

Cuban, L. (1986). *Teachers and machines: The classroom uses of technology since 1920.* New York: Teachers College Press.

Dewey, J. (1902/1956). The child and the curriculum. In J.A. Boydston (Ed.), *John Dewey: The middle works 1899–1924: Vol. 2: 1902–1903.* Carbondale: Southern Illinois University Press.

Fullan, M. (1991). *The new meaning of educational change.* New York: Teachers College Press.

Gardner, H. (1985). *The mind's new science: A history of the cognitive revolution.* New York: Basic Books.

Georgia State Department of Education. (1997). *Statewide educational technology plan: Blueprint.* Available on-line at: http://www.doe.k12.ga.us/downloads/StPlan97.pdf

Mississippi Department of Education. (1996). *Mississippi master plan for education technology.* Jackson: Mississippi Council for Education Technology and the Center for Educational Leadership and Technology. Available on-line at: http://www.mde.k12.ms.us/oet/pindex.html

Morine-Dershimer, G., & Corrigan, S. (1997). Teacher beliefs. In H.J. Walberg & G. D. Haertel (Eds.), *Psychology and educational practice.* Berkeley: CA: McCutchan Publishing Company.

National Research Council. (2000). *How people learn: Brain, mind, experience and school.* Committee on Developments in the Learning Sciences; Committee on Learning Research and Educational Practice. National Research Council. Washington, DC: National Academy Press.

Naughton, J. (1999). *A brief history of the future: The origins of the Internet.* London: Weidenfeld and Nicolson.

Noble, D.D. (1996). Mad rushes into the future: The overselling of educational technology. *Educational Technology, 54*(3), 18–23.

Office of Technology Assessment, Congress of the United States. (1995). *Teachers and technology: Making the connection.* Washington, DC: Office of Technology Assessment.

Resnick, L. (1987). *Education and learning to think.* Committee on Mathematics, Science, and Technological Education, Commission on Behavioral and Social Sciences and Education, National Research Council. Washington, DC: National Academy Press.

Roschelle, J.M., Pea, R.D., Hoadley, C.M., Gordon, D.N., & Means, B.M. (2000). Changing how and what children learn in school with computer-based technologies. *The Future of Children, 10,* 2, 76–101.

Sacks, O. (1995). Scotoma: Forgetting and neglecting in science. In R.B. Silvers (Ed.). *Hidden histories of science* (pp. 141–188). New York: New York Review of Books.

Sarason, S.B. (1993). *Revisiting "The culture of the school and the problem of change".* New York: Teachers College Press.

Schön, D. (1983). *The reflective practitioner: How professionals think in action.* New York: Basic Books.

Shavelson, R.J. (1976) Teacher's decision making. In N. Gage (Ed.). *The psychology of teaching methods.* Chicago: University of Chicago Press.

Shulman, L.S. (1987). Knowledge and teaching: Foundations of a new reform. *Harvard Educational Review, 57,* 1–22.

Shulman, L.S., & Quinlan, K. (1996). The comparative psychology of school subjects. In D.C. Berliner & R. Calfee (Eds.), *Handbook of educational psychology.* New York: Macmillan.

Texas Education Agency, 1996. *Long-range plan for technology, 1996–2010.* Available on-line at: http://www.tea.state.tx.us/

Zhao, Y. (1998). Design for adoption: Development of an integrated web-based education environment. *Journal of Research on Computing in Education, 30*(3), 307–328.

CHAPTER 3

EDUCATIONAL TECHNOLOGY STANDARDS FOR TEACHERS

Issues of Interpretation, Incorporation, and Assessment

Yong Zhao, Cindy Kendall, and Sophia H. Tan

INTRODUCTION

Over the past few years, an increasing number of states have begun to expect their teachers to be technologically proficient. In 1998, more than 80% of the 50 states required or recommended including a technology component in teacher education programs, up from only three states in 1995. In order to enforce and implement the requirement, state teacher certification agencies have also started to develop and adopt educational technology standards that spell out the specifics of the requirement. In 1998, nine states had teacher technology standards in place and another four states were in the process of developing teacher technology standards. Quite often, these standards are used as guidelines for assessing whether a teacher candidate has met the technology requirement sufficiently to be certified or whether a teacher education program is adequately preparing

What Should Teachers Know About Technology?: Perspectives and Practices, pages 31–44
Copyright © 2003 by Information Age Publishing

31

teachers to meet the state technology requirement. They are also used as the guiding framework for developing curriculum to help teacher candidates and practicing teachers to become technologically proficient and furthermore to include technology as a tool in the classroom. Therefore, state teacher technology standards are perhaps one of the most revealing sources for information about what teachers are expected to know about technology.

This paper reports the results of an analytical study of four states' technology standards and the most influential National Educational Technology Standards for Teachers (NETS.T) issued by ISTE, in collaboration with a number of agencies, including the United States Department of Education. The purpose of this study is both descriptive and evaluative. First, we try to describe what the standards are, that is to understand what concepts, knowledge, and skills in educational technology teachers are expected to possess. Second we try to evaluate the standards from three angles (a) are the standards easy to interpret?, (b) are the standards easy to incorporate?, and (c) is it easy to assess the implementation of the standards?

METHODS

Sample

We selected technology standards from four states for analysis—Connecticut, Colorado, Nebraska, and North Carolina. The primary reason for selecting these four states is that each of them represents a different time at which standards were published: North Carolina in 1995, when the Office of Technology Assessment released the first national report on technology and teachers; Connecticut in 1997, some time after the Office of Technology Assessment report; Colorado in 1999, right before ISTE released the National Educational Technology Standards for Teachers; and Nebraska in 2000, right after the release of NETS.T. Given that ISTE has been the leader in developing technology standards for teachers and many state standards were based on its first technology standards for teachers, we expect that the newly developed NETS.T, which is supported by the U.S. Department of Education, will have wide-reaching impact on future teacher technology standards. Thus, we also included NETS.T in our analysis.

Procedure

The two researchers first read the selected standards and formulated coding categories based on the research questions in order to examine the content of each standard. Coding categories included three main areas. The first was the Classification of the Standard. The researchers examined the perspective of the stated standard, determining whether the standard focused on a teacher technology skill or a classroom pedagogical application, and additionally what technologies were stated in the standard were also noted (word processing, spreadsheets, networks, etc.).

The second broad category was Orientation, with three possibilities. A standard with an Education Orientation described a teacher task and then tied in the technology tool. A standard with a Technology Orientation had a technology skill emphasized. Lastly, a standard with a Social Orientation focused on the ethical and legal impact of technology on teaching, learning and society. The researchers applied a binary measure of 1 or 0 to the Classification and Orientation measures of the standard.

The third and final category for coding was the Assessment of the Standard. The coding in this section used a Likert scale of 1–5, 1 = strongly disagree and 5 = strongly agree). The standards were assessed in three categories: interpretation, incorporation, and assessment of implementation. The question prompts used to examine the standards will be highlighted later in this chapter.

The coding was then conducted by one of the researchers and a graduate research assistant, who was not involved in the development of the coding scheme. The inter-rater consistency of all categories was 0.69. For each section, the inter-rater reliability of the Classification section was .97, and for the Orientation category .94 and for Assessment .52. It must be noted that the Classification and Orientation categories were simply a binary categorization (1, 0) and the Assessment category was on a 5-point Likert scale. There was not much variation in the scores by the raters in the Assessment category, but nonetheless there was more disagreement.

FINDINGS

Contents of Technology Standards

Overall, the four state technology standards and NETS.T are very similar in what they require teachers to do, although each standards document may take a different orientation in describing the content of the requirement. The contents of the standards include three basic types of components: (a) technological, (b) pedagogical, and (c) social, ethical, and legal. In other words, teachers are expected to possess certain technological skills and use them to improve teaching. Table 3.1 shows the major technological skills teachers are expected to have. It is obvious that teachers are expected to have knowledge of computer hardware and peripherals. Teachers are also expected to be able to troubleshoot hardware problems as well as install new software and upgrade computers. In terms of the software applications, teachers are expected to be able to use commonly available software packages in word processing/desktop publishing, database/spreadsheet, networking for file transfer and telecommunications (e.g., e-mail and the Internet), as well as multimedia (e.g., video, graphics, and audio).

Table 3.1.   Technological Skills Included in the Standards

	Hardware		Software/Application			
	Operation	Trouble-shooting	Word Processing Desktop Publishing	Database Spreadsheet	Networking Telecommuni-cation	Multi-media
Colorado	Yes	Yes	Yes	Yes	Yes	Yes
Connecticut	Yes	No	Yes	Yes	Yes	Yes
Nebraska	Yes	Yes	Yes	Yes	Yes	Yes
N Carolina	Yes	Yes	Yes	Yes	Yes	Yes
NETS.T	Yes	Yes	Yes	Yes	Yes	Yes

What differs across the standards is apparently not the content, but the orientation they take in describing the content and the degree of specificity of the requirement. Some standards (e.g., Colorado, North Carolina) are very specific in their description. The Colorado standards, for example, specify the exact discrete functions a teacher must be able to perform, such as "Insert and eject floppy disk and CD-ROM." (Colorado Department of Education, 1999). Other standards are more general. For example, the Nebraska standards require that "The educator is able to: use computer platforms to run programs; search for, access, generate, and manipulate data; print, publish, and communicate electronically" (Nebraska Department of Education, 2000, Educator Competency 1). This one standard includes and assumes a multitude of discrete functions. Even the Nebraska performance indicators are less specific than those of North Carolina. For instance, a Nebraska performance indicator asks that a teacher be able to use "basic computer operations such as editing, file management, printing, and multitasking" without specifying the specific functions. North Carolina and Colorado standards do not include performance indicators, as the performance of the task is explicit in the standard itself—no additional explanation is offered.

Definitions of Technology

It must be noted that although all standards use the term technology and that Table 3.1 may appear to suggest that all standards cover the same contents in technology, a closer look reveals subtle differences in what technological tools are considered important for teachers. None of the five sets of standards made any effort to define what technology means or what technological tools are considered. All seem to focus on computers, but other technology tools are also referred to within the standards documents. Among the states, there is a broad range of hardware and software included in the standards, demonstrating that there is considerable difference in interpretation of the word "technology." Table 3.2 lists the technological devices that are explicitly stated in the standards.

Table 3.2. Technological Devices Included in the Standards

Standards	Technology Definitions
Colorado	Computers and peripherals
Connecticut	Computers and peripherals, specific-purpose technology devices (graphing calculators, language translator, scientific probeware, electronic thesaurus)
Nebraska	Computers and computer-based technologies, scanners, projection devices, calculators, audio/video recorders and players, videodiscs, cameras, distant education systems
North Carolina	Computers and peripherals, videocassette recorder/player and monitor TV, video output devices

Besides the ability to use technological tools, the standards expect teachers to be able to integrate the use of technology tools and skills in their teaching and professional activities. Table 3.3 displays professional activities in which teachers are expected to use technology.

As Table 3.3 clearly shows, all standards we analyzed expect teachers to be able to use technology to access, evaluate, and select appropriate technologies and technology-based resources for instructional purposes. Teachers are also expected to integrate technology in their instruction to support student activities. Not all standards, however, list using technology to address the diverse needs of students. Most of the standards expect that the use of technology by teachers should help students to become technologically proficient. The differences are more pronounced when it comes to the expectations of teacher uses of technology for personal productivity and professional development.

Table 3.3. Technological Uses Included in the Standards

	Uses	CO	CT	NE	NC	NETS.T
Classroom applications	Access and select appropriate technologies and resources for teaching	Yes	Yes	Yes	Yes	Yes
	Use technology to support student activities	Yes	Yes	Yes	Yes	Yes
	Use technology to assess student learning	Yes	Yes	No	Yes	Yes
	Use technology to help students with special needs	Yes	No	No	Yes	Yes
	Use technology to help students develop technology competencies	No	Yes	Yes	Yes	Yes
	Manage classroom technology resources	No	No	No	Yes	Yes
Professional Uses	Use technology to engage in ongoing professional development	No	No	Yes	No	Yes
	Use technology to communicate with parents, colleagues, and students	No	No	Yes	No	Yes
	Use technology to increase personal productivity	No	No	Yes	No	Yes

The differences seem to be chronologically related. The more recent the standards are developed and released, the more categories they cover. In other words, it seems that more recent standards tend to expect teachers to use technology to do more things than some older standards, although they are in reality only a few years apart. In addition, more recent standards are shifting in focus from discrete technology skills to global technology-based tasks.

In addition to technical skills and the ability to use technology for instructional and professional development activities, some of the standards also expect teachers to master knowledge and model use concerning the social, legal, and ethical issues of technology. Although the specifics of these issues are described differently in the various standards, four out of the five standards examined (with the exception of Connecticut) have language concerning the social, legal, and ethical issues of technology use. The Colorado and North Carolina standards are much more narrow in their description of the issues than that of Nebraska and ISTE. The Colorado and North Carolina standards are solely concerned with policies and procedures of technology use in the schools while the former two are more focused on the broader impact that technology has on humanity and society, as well as general legal and ethical issues about technology.

Orientations of Technology Standards

We have identified three basic components in educational technology standards. In other words, the technology standards we have examined expect teachers to develop knowledge of and abilities in three possible areas: (a) technological, (b) pedagogical, and (c) social, ethical, and legal. As discussed in the previous section, not all standards expect teachers to be competent in all three areas. Neither do all standards place equal emphasis on all three areas. We found that the technology standards have different orientations. That is, some are more technology oriented in that they emphasize technical skills as their core requirement, while others may be education oriented in that they are more focused on the educational activities that a teacher may use technology to support and facilitate. Still, others can be more focused on the ethical and legal impact of technology teaching and learning. Orientation can also be understood as the framework within which the standards are presented. A technology-oriented standard starts from technology. The core contents of the standards are thus mostly about what technology knowledge teachers should have. On the other hand an education-oriented standard begins with the educational functions teachers perform. For example, the North Carolina standards are apparently technology oriented and include nine categories of knowledge and skills:

- Computer operation skills (e.g., "Identify and use icons, windows, menus").
- Setup, maintenance, and troubleshooting (e.g., "Protect and care for floppy disks").
- Word Processing/Introductory Desktop Publishing (e.g., "Check spelling, grammar, word usage").
- Spreadsheet/Graphing (e.g., "Entering data in an existing spreadsheet").
- Databases (e.g., "Insert database fields into word processing document").
- Networking (e.g., "Share files with others on a network").
- Telecommunications (e.g., "Access and use resources on the Internet and the World Wide Web").
- Media Communications (including image and audio processing) (e.g., "Produce electronic slides/overheads").
- Multimedia Integration (e.g., "Use a linear multimedia presentation").

In contrast, the National Educational Technology Standards for Teachers are certainly education oriented, the main categories focusing on educational rather than technological functions:

- Technology operations and concepts ("Teachers demonstrate a sound understanding of technology operations and concepts").
- Planning and designing learning environments and experiences ("Teachers plan and design effective learning environments and experiences supported by technology").
- Teaching, learning, and the curriculum ("Teachers implement curriculum plans that include methods and strategies for applying technology to maximize student learning").
- Assessment and evaluation ("Teachers apply technology to facilitate a variety of effective assessment and evaluation strategies").
- Productivity and professional practice ("Teachers use technology to enhance their productivity and professional practice").
- Social, ethical, legal, and human issues ("Teachers understand the social, ethical, legal, human issues surrounding the use of technology in PK–12 schools and apply that understanding in practice").

Obviously, the two standards have different orientations and foci. The orientations have significant impact on how the standards are achieved and assessed. We will return to this point later in our discussion. In our analysis, we identified an orientation to each of the subcategory or performance indicators of the standards. We then computed the percentage of orientations within each set of standards. For example, we found that every subcategory of the Colorado standards is technologically oriented, thus 100% of standards are technologically oriented, while only 33% of its indicators are education oriented. Table 3.4 summarizes the orientation of the five sets of standards we analyzed. The inter-rater consistency for the orientation section of our analysis is 94.74%, meaning that on nearly 95% of the occasions the two raters are consistent in their classification. Apparently the Colorado, Connecticut, and North Carolina standards have a greater technology orientation, while the NETS.T and Nebraska standards are more oriented to educational functions in terms of contents.

Table 3.4. Orientations of the Standards

Orientation	CO (%)	CT (%)	NE (%)	NC (%)	NETS.T (%)
Technology	100	100	92	100	57
Education	33	33	62	50	65
Social Issues	33	33	23	14	32

ASSESSING THE STANDARDS

The previous sections provided an overview of the contents of technology standards. We now turn to the qualities of the standards. As mentioned before, we measured the quality of the standards with three scales: *Interpretability, Incorporability*, and *Assessibility*. Each of these terms will be discussed in our findings below.

Interpretability

For standards to be useful, they must be easy to understand. That is, it should be easy for different people to reach consistent interpretations of what they mean. Interpretability can be defined as the ease with which the educator can interpret the published standard. The standards are rated on a 1 to 5 Likert scale (1 being "Strongly disagree," and 5 being "Strongly agree") with regard to the following three questions:

1. It is easy for the teacher to know what he or she should do to meet the standard.
2. It is easy for a third party to judge to what degree the teacher has met the standard.
3. It is easy for a Teacher Education Institution to develop a program or curriculum to prepare teacher candidates to meet this standard.

Of particular interest is the choice of the word "easy" in the above questions. One of our research questions deals with the interpretation of the published standard, in other words the apparent ease of interpretation of the standard by the intended audience of the standard.

An additional question was also asked in this section, related to the number of interpretations possible of each particular standard:

4. Does the standard provoke single or multiple interpretations? (Responses were coded either S or M.)

Table 3.5 summarizes the ratings for each set of standards.

There are several points worth highlighting here. First, the four state standards fared well in terms of how easy it is for teachers and others to know if they are meeting the standards. In other words, the standards are specific enough for teachers and others to know what is required and whether they have the required skills. The Colorado standards rank the highest, while the lowest is the NETS.T. Second, the standards that rated high in terms of interpretability seem to be those with a stronger technology orientation, while the ones that rated lower are more oriented toward

Table 3.5.   Interpretability Ratings of Standards

Question	CO n=3		CT n=3		NE n=13		NC n=14		NETS.T n=16	
	Mean	SD	Mean	SD	Mean	SD	Mean	SD	Mean	SD
1	5.00	0.00	4.00	0.00	4.00	0.00	4.57	0.65	3.91	1.00
2	5.00	0.00	4.00	0.00	4.00	0.00	4.64	0.50	4.22	0.42
3	5.00	0.00	4.00	0.00	4.00	0.00	3.86	0.36	3.57	0.99
4	67%	33%	67%	33%	67%	33%	67%	33%	100%	0%

1. For questions 1 through 3, the numbers are the means and standard deviations, while for question 4, they represent the percentage of sub-standards allowing for single (S) or multiple (M) interpretations

2. For questions 1 through 3, 5 = "Strongly agree" and 1 = "Strongly disagree"

n = number of standards analyzed

educational functions. This difference suggests that it is easier to put forward specific standards in terms of technological skills, rather than the ability to use technology for educational purposes. Of course, simplicity and specificity do not necessarily equate to desirability. In other words, the standards that specify exactly what technological devices and functions teachers must master are not necessarily better in terms of educational outcomes. While a teacher may know how to use a CD-ROM, he may not know how to use it effectively in his teaching. We will return to this point later in the discussion section. The third obvious point is that the degree of specificity corresponds well with the degree of ease for a program to develop a curriculum to prepare teachers to meet the standard. That is, the more specific and explicit a standard is, the easier it is for teacher education programs to teach to it.

Incorporability

While interpretability of a standard measures its specificity and exclusivity of multiple interpretations, the incorporability indicates to what degree the standards can be easily integrated in the existing curriculum of a teacher or a teacher education program. Incorporability is an important consideration because it directly affects the feasibility of implementation of a standard. Teachers are already overloaded and do not have time to learn new technologies. Thus, unless they can incorporate the required technology into their current curriculum, it is difficult for them to learn it. Likewise, the curriculum for teacher education is already quite full. Adding a technology requirement means taking time away from other important curricula components. Hence, it is important for what is required in technology standards to be easily incorporated into the existing curriculum.

To assess the incorporability of the standards, we used a Likert scale (1 to 5) to rate the standards on two questions (1 = Strongly disagree, 5 = Strongly agree):

1. It is easy for the teacher to incorporate this standard into the curriculum.

2. It is easy for a Teacher Education Institution to incorporate this standard into its existing curriculum.

Table 3.6 shows the means and standard deviations of the ratings.

Table 3.6.   Incorporability Ratings of Standards

	CO n=3		CT n=3		NE n=13		NC n=14		NETS.T n=16	
Question	Mean	SD	Mean	SD	Mean	SD	Mean	SD	Mean	SD
1	5.00	0.00	4.00	0.00	4.00	0.00	4.00	0.00	3.96	0.88
2	5.00	0.00	4.00	0.00	4.00	0.00	3.70	0.44	3.48	0.90

It seems apparent that the Colorado standards have very high incorporability—it is easy for teachers to incorporate them into their existing curriculum and for teacher education institutions to include them in the existing curriculum. On the other hand, the NETS.T is much more difficult in both regards. Again, when the standards are more concerned about technological skills and knowledge, it is easier for them to be incorporated because they are more specific and better defined. In contrast, when standards are less defined and specific, they are more difficult to implement.

Assessibility of Implementation

After individual teachers or teacher education institutions begin to implement technology standards, it is necessary to find ways to assess to what degree the implementation is faithful and on the right track. Therefore, we rated the potential apparent assessibility of implementation of the standards using the following questions on a Likert scale (5 = strongly agree, 1 = strongly disagree):

1. It is easy for the teacher to assess the implementation of this standard.

2. It is easy for a third party to assess the implementation of this standard.

3. It is easy for the Teacher Education Institution to assess the implementation of this standard.

Table 3.7 displays the mean ratings of the accessibility of the standards.

Table 3.7. Assessibility Ratings of Standards

| Question | CO n=3 | | CT n=3 | | NE n=13 | | NC n=14 | | NETS.T n=16 | |
	Mean	SD	Mean	SD	Mean	SD	Mean	SD	Mean	SD
1	5.00	0.00	4.33	0.47	4.00	0.00	4.64	0.50	4.52	0.73
2	5.00	0.00	4.33	0.47	4.00	0.00	4.57	0.51	4.00	0.00
3	5.00	0.00	4.33	0.47	4.00	0.00	4.64	0.50	4.00	0.00

Surprisingly all standards received good ratings, suggesting that it is easy during initial reading and interpretation of the standards to assess whether the standards are implemented faithfully. Again, the Colorado standards stand out as the one that received the highest rating. Even the NETS.T received relatively high ratings, especially when compared with the ratings it received in the other two areas.

DISCUSSION

Thus far, we have presented the results of our analysis of the five technology standards for teachers. We found that the standards include three domains of concepts, knowledge, and skills: technological, pedagogical, and social/ethical. We also found that technology standards can be written with certain orientations. Some of the standards we analyzed are more concerned about the technological functions a teacher can perform, while others are more focused on the educational functions teachers can perform with technology. Furthermore, we found that the technology standards have varying degrees of interpretability and incorporability, although they all seem to fare well in terms of the ease of assessing their implementation. These findings, however, need to be further discussed to avoid any misleading conclusions. In the following paragraphs, we discuss these findings in the context of a number of pressing issues surrounding teacher learning and use of technology.

Using Technology versus Using Technology to Teach

As mentioned before, technology standards can adopt different orientations. They can be focused on technological knowledge, concepts, and skills. Standards following this orientation define what teachers should know in terms of technological functions teachers need to perform and specify what technological devices and software applications teachers should learn to use. In other words, the standards are concerned with each teacher's ability to use technology. In contrast, educational technology standards can have an education orientation. Standards with this orientation define what teachers should know in terms of educational functions teachers can perform with the support of technology. They are concerned with teachers' ability to use technology as a tool for many different teacher tasks, such as classroom instruction, interaction with colleagues and parents, and professional development.

It seems reasonable to believe that education-oriented standards are more desirable than technology-oriented standards since the ultimate goal for teachers to learn about technology is to improve education through technology. However, it is ironic that education-oriented standards seem to be of different quality when it comes to interpretability and incorporability, as they are less easy to implement, incorporate, and assess. As our findings demonstrate, technology-oriented standards tend to afford individuals clear and specific understandings of what is expected and how to go about meeting the requirement. It is also the case that, the more specific technology-oriented standards appear to be easier for teachers and teacher education programs to incorporate in their teaching.

This finding is not surprising, yet it is worth noting because it reveals the complexity and messiness of the business of standards-setting. Policy makers tend to favor the specific, explicit, clear-cut, and unambiguous requirement that can be measured easily. Practitioners tend to favor them as well because it is purely simpler to add isolated technological modules or courses than reforming established practices to integrate technology, so as to help teachers develop the ability to use technology to teach. However, technological competency does not automatically translate into pedagogical solutions. The ability to use technology does not equal the ability to use technology to teach. Thus, merely requiring teachers to learn to use certain devices or software will not automatically result in improved teaching. How to balance between enough technology knowledge (skills) and knowledge to teach with technology (pedagogy), thus becomes crucial for those who set standards, as well those who implement them.

Specificity versus Generality

When we analyzed the standards, we sensed a common dilemma faced by the developers of these standards. On the one hand, standards need to be specific so that they can be interpreted correctly, assessed easily, and implemented faithfully. On the other hand, standards cannot be too specific, especially in the technology arena because if they are overly specific, they become rigid and outdated very quickly due to the rapid change of technology and diverse ways to achieve the same functionality. For example, the convergence of media has made the Web a potential technology for a variety of tasks: word processing, database, spreadsheet, video, audio, presentation, e-mail, and publishing can all be done within a web-based application. Thus, a standard that specifies applications may already be outdated and finding the appropriate level of specificity becomes yet another demanding task for both standards makers and implementers.

REFERENCES

Alliance of Regional Educational Service Centers and Connecticut State Department of Education. (1997). *Technology competencies for Connecticut educators.* Hartford, CT: Alliance of Regional Educational Service Centers and Connecticut State Department of Education.

Colorado Department of Education. (1999). *Colorado technology competency guidelines for classroom teachers and school library media specialists.* Denver: Colorado Department of Education.

Education Week. (1998). *Technology counts '98: Putting school technology to the test* (Special Report). Washington, DC: Author. http://www.edweek.org/sreports/tc98/

International Society for Technology in Education. (1991). *ISTE recommended foundations in technology for all teachers.* Eugene, OR: Author.

Nebraska Department of Education. (2000). *Nebraska educator competencies in technology.* Omaha: Author.

North Carolina Department of Public Instruction. (1995). *Technology competencies for educators.* Raleigh: Author.

U.S. Congress Office of Technology Assessment. (1995). *Teachers and technology: Making the connection* (OTA-EHR-616). Washington, DC: Author.

CHAPTER 4

TECHNOLOGY AS MEDIA

A Learner-Centered Perspective

James A. Levin and Bertram C. Bruce

INTRODUCTION

Why Learn?

It may be somewhat heretical to raise this question, but why do or should people learn? To make this a plausible question, let us enumerate some of the costs of learning.

Costs of Learning

There are at least six costs of learning:

1. Learning takes time and effort by the learner. Not only are there direct costs to the learner and the society that the learner belongs to, but there are also opportunity costs. The time and effort spent on learning are time and effort that are not spent on other things, especially in our current school system in which learning is isolated from doing.

What Should Teachers Know About Technology?: Perspectives and Practices, pages 45–51
Copyright © 2003 by Information Age Publishing
All rights of reproduction in any form reserved.

2. Learning can also interfere (at least temporarily) with the performance of previously acquired expertise.

3. Learning also requires the time and effort of others (teachers, mentors, others involved in the support of learning), again with both direct and opportunity costs.

4. Learning can lead to the disruption of group performance, again at least temporarily. The introduction of new knowledge or skills can impair the performance of an efficiently operating group.

5. Learning consumes some of the resources of society, and thus competes against other demands on society's resources.

6. Learning can lead to the disruption of social relations and the social structure of society, at least until a new equilibrium is reached.

Benefits of Learning

Now that we have seen the costs of learning, we can of course enumerate the benefits. Learning allows individuals, groups, and societies to adapt to changing contexts much faster and much more effectively than other mechanisms (evolution, for example).

Balance Between Learning and Doing

If we had a society in which nobody learned anything, there would be no good way for that society and the individuals in it to be able to adapt to rapid changes in the environment, and so the society would collapse when faced with significant changes faster than evolution operates and the individuals would die.

On the other extreme, if we had a society in which individuals always learned and never performed, then the society would not produce the necessities of life and again would collapse. So we can see that there is a need for a balance between learning and doing, in which the benefits of learning outweigh the costs of learning.

That balance can be impacted by the media available for learning. As the media change, then the costs of learning can change and the benefits of learning also can change. Let us look at a range of media, and examine in some depth the ways that they impact learners.

MEDIA FOR LEARNING:
A REPRESENTATIONAL TOOLKIT MODEL FOR EXPERTISE

What does it mean to have learned something? Over the past 20 years, there has been a series of studies of what distinguishes experts in a domain from novices (Chi, Feltovich, & Glaser, 1981; Chi, Glaser, & Farr, 1988; Larkin, McDermott, Simon, & Simon, 1980). In a number of different domains, the findings are consistent—experts have multiple ways of thinking about the domain, while novices have only one or a few ways. Experts have many different representations of the knowledge domain, they can switch from one representation to another, and they have the meta-knowledge that allows them to know which representation to choose for which task and which representation to switch to while solving the task.

When an expert accomplishes a task smoothly, he uses this meta-knowledge to select an appropriate initial representation for the task, typically a global, qualitative representation. The expert proceeds until meta-knowledge indicates the value of switching to another representation, often more detailed and sometimes more quantitative (depending on the domain). Finally, the expert completes the task, after perhaps more switches of representations.

When an expert encounters a problem, he uses this meta-knowledge to switch to a different representation that may allow the expert to overcome the problem. If not, then the expert switches to yet another representation, until either the problem is solved or the expert has applied all representations.

One model for thinking about expertise in this way is the Representational Toolkit framework (Levin, Stuve, & Jacobson, 1999). An expert craftsman has a range of different tools, with skill at using each tool, as well as knowledge of when to sequentially use each tool, in order to accomplish a task. Similarly, an expert in a knowledge domain has a range of different knowledge representations, and the meta-knowledge of which representation to use at different times. Debates about which is the "best" representation of a knowledge domain, in this model, may be similar to arguments about which is the "best" tool, a hammer or a saw.

IMPLICATIONS FOR THE DESIGN
OF LEARNING ENVIRONMENTS

What are the implications of this way of thinking about expertise for designing learning environments? One implication is that learning environments should be designed to help learners acquire multiple representations of the domain area. A second implication is that learning environments should help learners acquire skill at switching between one representation and another. In other words, the representations should be coordinated. A third implication is that learning environments should help learners acquire meta-knowledge about these representations, including the meta-knowledge of when to use each representation and when to stop using it and instead switch to another.

One of the strengths of new computer-based technologies is that they can display to the learner multiple presentations of knowledge in a domain to the learner at the same time, in a way that is coordinated. In other words, an action by the learner on one representation is automatically reflected in changes in all the other presentations. These multiple coordinated presentations can then support the acquisition of multiple coordinated representations. But how can we systematically think about multiple presentations, given the diversity of knowledge domains?

A TAXONOMY OF USES OF TECHNOLOGIES FOR LEARNING

Bruce and Levin (2003, 1997) proposed a taxonomy of uses of technologies for learning based on the natural impulses of a child proposed by John Dewey (1943): inquiry, communication, construction, and expression. In this taxonomy, the diversity of uses of technologies for learning is captured by these four different media for learning, based on the goals of the learner. Could this same framework help us to systematically think about the diversity of knowledge domains and therefore help us to construct learning environments that support the development of expertise? To explore this, let us examine each of the four categories to see.

Media for Inquiry

Technologies can be used as media for learning through inquiry. The inquiry-based learning framework focuses on this particular set of uses. Innovative learning approaches in science, mathematics, and engineering have concentrated on this set of uses (Bruce & Levin, 1997).

Inquiry can be used as the basis of a presentation mode. One example is the Inquiry Page (http://inquiry.uiuc.edu), a web-based portal of resources focusing on inquiry learning. Many other presentations are inquiry-oriented, especially those designed for science. The best examples of these science inquiry environments are the "workbench" web sites, for example, the Biology Workbench (http://workbench.sdsc.edu/) and the Biology Student Workbench (http://bioweb.ncsa.uiuc.edu/). These were set up explicitly to facilitate inquiry processes, including the search of multiple databases and the analyses of retrieved datasets.

Media for Communication

Technologies can also be used as media for learning through communication. Teaching, for example, is a specialized form of communication, and many of the existing and new technologies have served to support learning through teaching. There are also other communicative uses of technology that can support learning. Communication with other learners or communication with others outside the current educational system is one example. Many of the innovative approaches to the use of new technologies for learning in the language arts have focused on media for communication (Bruce & Levin, 2001).

Many innovative uses of technologies for learning have been communication presentations. Most of the "course package" web systems (WebCT, Blackboard, WebBoard) explicitly present a communicative model. There are various forms of communication available within such a system: conferences, homework drop-boxes, announcement sections, test sections, lectures, and lecture note, which are all forms of communication. Collaborative learning, especially that learning mediated through new technologies (computer-supported collaborative learning or CSCL), is another cutting-edge approach to learning.

Media for Construction

Technologies can be used as media for learning through construction. The current constructivist approaches emphasize knowledge construction. In fact, the new "constructionist" approach explicitly focuses on the construction of external artifacts as important for learning (Kafai & Resnick, 1996). Even for older problem-based learning and project-based learning approaches, construction (either individually or jointly) plays a major role in learning. Several uses of innovative technologies for learning have taken a "construction set" presentation mode. In this mode, the user is presented with a set of "parts," and constructs entities by selecting parts and combining them to create some new computational object. For example, the whole range of simulation building educational environments function as construction sets, with the person learning through building—whether building a city, a world, a physics experiment, or an ant colony. Once built, these constructions then "run," and the person learns by observing the results of their particular construction.

Media for Expression

Technologies can be used as media for learning through expression. This is a fairly frequent use of new technologies in the language arts (Bruce & Levin, 2001). Much of the focus of theories of writing and other creative arts deals with the development of one's own voice (Graves, 1983), which is a focus on self-expression.

One of the first tools developed for modern graphic interfaces was a series of painting and drawing programs (PaintPot from Xerox PARC; MacPaint from Apple). Computer-based photo editing, music editing, and video editing applications are examples of new technologies oriented toward expression.

SUMMARY

By examining both the costs and benefits of learning, we can see the impact that new technologies for learning have on the learner, the learning environment, and the larger society. The learner-based taxonomy of technology uses for learning, when combined with emerging theories of the nature of expertise, provides a basis for systematically designing more powerful contexts for learning.

REFERENCES

Bruce, B.C. (2001). The Inquiry Page: A collaboratory for curricular innovation. *Learning Technology, 3*(1).

Bruce, B., & Levin, J. (2003). Roles for new technologies in language arts: Inquiry, communication, construction, and expression. In J. Jenson, J. Flood, D. Lapp, & J. Squire (Eds.), *The handbook for research on teaching the language arts.* Macmillan.

Bruce, B.C., & Levin, J.A. (1997). Educational technology: Media for inquiry, communication, construction, and expression. *Journal of Educational Computing Research, 17*(1), 79–102.

Chi, M.T.H., Feltovich, P.J., & Glaser, R. (1981). Categorization and representation of physics problems by experts and novices. *Cognitive Science, 5,* 121–152.

Chi, M.T.H., Glaser, R., & Farr, M.J. (Eds.). (1988). *The nature of expertise.* Hillsdale, NJ: Lawrence Erlbaum Associates.

Dewey, J. (1943). *The child and the curriculum: The school and society.* Chicago: University of Chicago Press.

Graves, D.H. (1983). *Writing: Teachers and children at work.* Portsmouth, NH: Heinemann Educational Books.

Kafai, Y.B., & Resnick, M. (1996). *Constructionism in practice: Designing, thinking, and learning in a digital world.* Mahwah, NJ: Lawrence Erlbaum Associates.

Larkin, J.H., McDermott, J., Simon, D.P., & Simon, H.A. (1980). Expert and novice performance in solving physics problems. *Science, 208,* 1335–1342.

Levin, J.A., Stuve, M.J., & Jacobson, M.J. (1999). Teachers' conceptions of the Internet and the World Wide Web: A representational toolkit as a model of expertise. *Journal of Educational Computing Research, 21*(1), 1–23.

CHAPTER 5

FLUENCY WITH INFORMATION TECHNOLOGY

The Computer Science Perspective

Mark Urban-Lurain

INTRODUCTION

What should teachers know about information technology from the perspective of the discipline of computer science (CS)? Computer science faculties have not traditionally addressed the question of what *teachers* should know about computer science. However, they have grappled with the general question of what non-computer science students should know about computing for many years. In this chapter, I discuss the history of computer science courses for non-computer science college students. I summarize the recent recommendations about Fluency with Information Technology from the Computer Science and Telecommunications Board of the National Research Council. I then outline the instructional design of the Computing Concepts and Competencies course at Michigan State University that we created to prepare students to be Fluent with Information Technology and discuss the innovative assessments we use to evaluate stu-

What Should Teachers Know About Technology?: Perspectives and Practices, pages 53–74
Copyright © 2003 by Information Age Publishing
All rights of reproduction in any form reserved.

dent outcomes and the methods we use to validate the course design and assessments. Finally, I discuss the implications for preparing teachers to use information technology in their practice.

TRENDS IN INTRODUCTORY CS COURSES FOR NON-CS MAJORS

Computer science is a relatively young and fast changing discipline. Until the late 1970s, computing was done on large mainframe computers and only specially trained personnel were allowed to *use* computers. In K–12 schools, when computers were used, they were used for business and administrative purposes. Since computers were not used for instruction, teachers had no need to know about information technology.

During this time, undergraduate students learned about computing by learning to program. Non-computer science students may have taken one or two courses to learn FORTRAN or COBOL. Since computing resources were very scarce and students were not able to create very large or useful programs, the primary goal was to give students a sense of how computers worked and what kinds of tasks they could perform. Given the ways that these students were expected to use computers, this curriculum made sense. Because K–12 teachers did not use computers, few teacher education students took these early computer science courses.

With the advent of microcomputers, computing technology rapidly moved from the traditional roles of management information systems, to playing a central role in the regular work of many disciplines where it had previously had little, if any, impact. In the K–12 arena, some teachers began to use this new technology for classroom management tasks such as writing and keeping student records. Soon, some early adopters began to incorporate computers into their instruction. Because these teachers were interested in computers, preparing them to use the technology was not an issue. They were eager to experiment with the new technology and willing to endure the problems associated with trial and error learning. However, as school districts increased funding to place information technology into more classrooms, the question of how to prepare teachers to use this technology effectively became part of the policy debate.

The widespread influx of information technology across a variety of disciplines caused increased demand in most colleges and universities for courses that would prepare students from a variety of majors to use information technology effectively in their disciplines. In many schools, the task of preparing these students to use information technology fell to the computer science departments.

To understand the trends in computer science courses designed for non-CS students, Urban-Lurain and Weinshank (2001) reviewed the conference proceedings of the two primary conferences for computer science education: the National Educational Computing Conference (NECC) and Association for Computing Machinery Special Interest Group on Computer Science Education (ACM SIGCSE). The literature from 1979 to 1998 shows clear trends away from teaching programming to non-CS students. In the decade between 1979 and 1988, 52% of the courses described in these articles had a programming focus. However, the number of courses with programming as the primary emphasis has decreased recently. From 1990 to 1998, only 36% of the courses for non-computer science majors had a programming focus, with a downward trend during that time. During this time, more courses emphasized computer applications, "computer literacy" and surveys of the discipline of computer science. By 1998, there were no articles about non-major courses in which the primary focus was programming. In that year, the emphasis in the literature was on managing the rapidly increasing enrollment demands in these courses due to growing institutional requirements for technological competence among students across a wide variety of disciplines.

Fluency With Information Technology

This demand for broader technological education in colleges and universities reflects a national trend. In 1997, the Computer Science and Telecommunications Board (CSTB) of the National Research Council (NRC) formed a committee to make recommendations about information literacy. The committee's report, *Being Fluent with Information Technology* (Committee on Information Technology Literacy, 1999), introduces the term *Fluency with Information Technology* (FIT). Persons who are FIT move beyond "training" to a deeper level of conceptual understanding that allows them to use their knowledge of information technology to solve new problems in different domains and to learn to use new software as it becomes available. According to the report, FITness requires three types of knowledge: (a) contemporary information technology skills; (b) foundational concepts of computer science; and (c) intellectual capabilities. The report identifies ten elements for each of the three types of knowledge that constitute FITness.

Information Technology Skills

A FIT person must have the ability to use various computer applications. However, these skills change rapidly with the changes in technology. The ten skills identified by the committee are all necessary for teachers who will need to use information technology. These include the following:

1. Setting up a personal computer—knowing the major components; understanding how to connect them and configure them to operate.

2. Using basic operating system features—installing and operating software, managing disk and file resources.

3. Using a word processor to create a text document—organize and edit documents and include data, such as images, from other sources.

4. Using a graphics and/or artwork package—create illustrations, slides, or other image-based expressions of ideas.

5. Connecting a computer to a network—understanding the various types of network connectivity options.

6. Using the Internet to find information and resources—being able to effectively use search engines and evaluate the quality of the results.

7. Using a computer to communicate with others—electronic mail is the most current form, but the use of other collaborative and communication software is increasing.

8. Using a spreadsheet to model simple processes or financial tables—understanding how to design and create the appropriate formulas for the specified task.

9. Using a database—setting up and accessing useful information.

10. Using instructional materials to learn how to use new applications or features—with the rapid changes in software, the ability to learn new software from the help system and other instructional materials is crucial.

Information Technology Concepts

The FITness report notes that "computer literacy" has come to be associated with simply training people on sets of inert skills. In contrast, FITness requires knowledge of the principles and concepts of computing that form the basis of computer science. By understanding the deeper concepts, persons who are FIT can adapt to new computing environments and cope with the unexpected when using information technology. The ten most important concepts identified by the committee include the following:

1. Computers—the idea that computer software is a deterministic set of instructions telling the computer what to do for a given set of input.

2. Information systems—the general structure of hardware, software, people and processes, interfaces and their abstract structure.

3. Networks—understanding how information is routed among computers connected to networks and how different parameters impact the responsiveness and usability of the network for various tasks.

4. Digital representation of information—the general concept of all computer representation being encoded in some binary form and that all information processing involves reading and transforming the various data representations.

5. Information organization—which includes various information formats, classification, searching and retrieving and assessing information quality.

6. Modeling and abstraction—understanding the notions of how models approximate reality and that the model is not reality.

7. Algorithmic thinking and programming—because information technology is based upon programming, this concept is essential to understanding how and why information systems work as they do.

8. Universality—the idea that any computer may perform any computation task, the only limits are the speed and ease with which any particular computer can perform the task.

9. Limitations of information technology—knowing what computers can—and cannot—do is critical to being able to determine how information technology can be applied to the solution of a problem.

10. Societal impact of information and information technology—the technical basis for concerns about privacy, intellectual property, mediated social interactions and the implications for social policies in these areas.

Intellectual Capabilities

Finally, FITness requires the ability to apply information technology in particular contexts and to use information technology to solve new problems. FITness requires greater general intellectual capabilities that all teachers should have, including the ability to do the following:

1. Engage in sustained reasoning—defining and clarifying a problem to the level of specificity required to solve it using information technology.

2. Manage complexity—understanding the relative advantages and disadvantages of different solutions to problems and organizing the resources necessary to solve problems effectively.

3. Test a solution—determining when a given solution meets the design requirements of a problem.

4. Manage problems in faulty solutions—detecting, diagnosing and correcting problems in a logical fashion.

5. Organize and navigate information structures and evaluate information—finding the information needed to solve a problem and evaluating the relevance and quality of the information in a given context.

6. Collaborate—knowing how to use information technology to facilitate collaboration with colleagues in ways not possible without the information technology.

7. Communicate with other audiences—using technology to effectively communicate requires knowledge of the communication process and how to use technology to enhance, rather than detract from, the communication.

8. Expect the unexpected—the use of technology often has unexpected consequences because the technology is embedded in a larger social and technical context.

9. Anticipate changing technologies—users must be able to understand and weigh the benefits and costs of new technologies when deciding which to adopt and when to do so.

10. Think about information technology abstractly—identifying common principles and using them to transfer technical solutions from one situation to another.

The committee notes that the contemporary skills will change quickly over time, with the advances of computer software, while the underlying computing concepts are more stable. Intellectual capabilities should not be restricted to a single course but should be developed throughout the undergraduate curriculum. Therefore, teachers should learn both skills with applications and the computing concepts and principles so that they can use computers to solve problems in a variety of disciplines.

FITNESS AT MICHIGAN STATE UNIVERSITY

While this definition of FITness is one that many can support, the FITness report stops short of making specific curriculum recommendations to implement these goals. This rest of this chapter summarizes how in the Department of Computer Science and Engineering at Michigan State University teaches FITness.

The Importance of Conceptual Understanding

As the FITness report asserts, conceptual understanding is critical if people are going to transfer their knowledge about technology to new contexts and adapt to rapidly changing information technology. Traditionally, introductory computer science courses have taught computer programming as the principle conceptual foundation of computer science. Programming was a critical part of FITness because all interactions with computers required programming (e.g., Rodriguez & Anger, 1981). However, interaction with information technology has now moved to higher levels of abstraction. For example, collecting and analyzing data used to require writing computer programs; today we use spreadsheets and databases to do these tasks with much greater ease and sophistication. As computer software evolved and programming was no longer a necessary "skill" for using computers, some computer science faculty justified teaching programming as a way to develop general problem-solving skills (e.g., Tu & Johnson, 1990). However, as Urban-Lurain and Weinshank (2000) point out, learning theory calls into question the idea that learning to program develops generic problem-solving skills.

Deep understanding requires mental models or schemas of information systems. To teach these, many courses for non-CS majors take a deductive approach adapted from the curriculum for CS majors. They present abstract computing concepts to students with the goal of having students (a) learn the concepts, (b) learn to identify a variety of disparate computing problems, (c) link the problems to the underlying concepts, and (d) apply the concepts to the solution of the problems. This is a long chain of inference that has rarely been successful in courses for non-CS majors.

Our experience teaching non-CS majors was that both skills-only and programming-plus-applications approaches failed (Weinshank, Urban-Lurain, Danieli, & McCuaig, 1992; Weinshank, Urban-Lurain, Danieli, & McCuaig, 1995). Our students often arrived in their subsequent courses unable to perform any but the most rudimentary computing tasks. They had not retained what they had learned with either approach and could not transfer their knowledge to comparable problems in their disciplines. Students who had learned particular keystrokes in specific applications software did not have the necessary conceptual understanding to segue into new software environments. On the other hand, students who had learned programming could not see the applicability of the programming constructs to the problems they were trying to solve. This is because programming constructs (e.g., control structures and variables) are too far removed from the concepts that learners need to transfer their knowledge to using application software to solve problems (e.g., hierarchical file systems, data representation.)

Design of the Computing Concepts and Competencies Course

In the summer of 1996, we set out to design a new introductory CS course for non-CS majors with the goal of building upon what we had learned in our previous efforts.[1] We began by conducting a series of interviews with the chairs and faculty representatives of the 67 client departments whose students would take the new course to identify the computing competencies and skills that are important for each major in their future courses and careers. The client departments' needs were consistent with many of the principles of FITness: they wanted students to be able to use computers to solve a variety of different problems across a variety of domains throughout the curriculum and into their careers. Since computing systems and software are changing rapidly, the departments wanted their students to be able to adapt to new computing systems and use them for solving new problems. Although understanding computing concepts is critical to meet these goals, we knew that the traditional instructional approaches that we had used were longer viable. This meant that we had to develop a new approach to teaching computing concepts.

Teaching Concepts Inductively

Rather than teaching students decontextualized concepts and then expecting them to apply those concepts to solve problems, we decided to use an inductive approach. Students solve a series of problems that we have chosen because they epitomize classes of problems representative of the various computing concepts (Reigeluth & Stein, 1983). As students grapple with problems that may appear to be unrelated, the instruction must tie the problems together, showing students how each problem is an example of particular concepts or principles. Students can then "triangulate" on these concepts and principles, refining their schemas as they solve successively more abstract problems, allowing their novice knowledge to evolve into expert knowledge (Smith, diSessa, & Roschelle, 1993). Figure 5.1 represents the process.

Students learn *Skill 1* (represented by the smaller circle) and build a mental schema representing a generalization of this particular skill (indicated by the larger circle, *Schema 1*). This schema may consist of accurate representations of the computing concepts along with misconceptions. Students then learn subsequent skills and build corresponding schemas. The intersection of these schemas triangulates on more accurate representations of the *concept* (Anderson, 1984; Shuell, 1986). As students learn an increasing number of discrete skills, understanding how these skills are instantiations of the underlying concepts reduces the cognitive load required to represent the knowledge, as compared with the requirements of storing an increasing number of discrete, unrelated skills (Chandler & Sweller, 1991). The goal is for the students' conceptual understanding to become rich enough to allow them to apply the concepts to independent

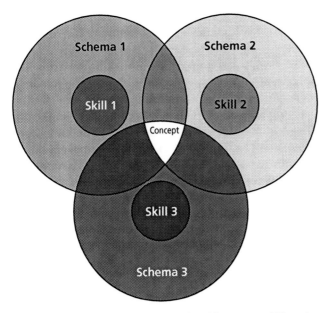

Figure 5.1.   Concept map of relationship among skills, schema, and concepts.

problem solving beyond that which is possible with solely procedural skills. This approach not only engenders improved conceptual development, but also enhances retention and transfer (Foshay, 1991).

Although developing a set of computing skills is a necessary condition for this approach, it is not sufficient. It is crucial to maintain the importance of computing concepts in the instruction. To do so, we use a spiral curriculum (Bruner, 1960) to present increasingly challenging problems that require students to synthesize the apparently discrete skills they are learning. Constantly recapitulating key concepts helps students comprehend the utility and importance of understanding the computing concepts for the practical requirements of adapting to new and changing software.

Multiple "Tracks"

After analyzing our client department needs, we identified a set of "core" computing competencies that appeared to be common across the university. These included (a) the basic functions of an operating system; (b) hierarchical file structures; (c) computer networking (e-mail, the Web, distributed file systems); (d) the ability search for and make sense of information from a variety of sources; and (e) the ability to use word processing software to create large documents and reports. Beyond the core competencies, various departments had different requirements. Some wanted their students to be able to create more elaborate reports and presentations; some wanted their students to be able to perform sophisticated data analysis; and some wanted their students to use computers for financial and business applications.

Given the different applications required by the various departments, we decided that a single, monolithic course would not meet the needs of all of the clients. While the underlying computing concepts are similar across domains (e.g., using parameters to allow the computer to take different actions depending on the values of parameters) the instantiation of these concepts varies across applications. For example, web pages can be used to teach parameters by exploring the effects of changing parameters in the HTML tags for Java applets. Students can use spreadsheets to see the effects of changing function parameters on the resulting calculations. Multiple tracks allow students to learn the underlying concepts in a context that is useful to their majors. This approach maintains student interest and motivation, a key factor for learning (Keller, 1983; Yelon, 1996).

Collaborative, Problem-Based Learning

Because this is an introductory course for which there are no prerequisites, incoming students have a wide range of computing knowledge and experience. This presents a number of instructional challenges such as (a) ascertaining and keeping pace with changing incoming student experience, (b) maintaining motivation among the more experienced students, and (c) ensuring that novice students do not become discouraged or fall behind. We used collaborative learning to address these challenges. Each day the students are randomly assigned to groups of two to four so that they work with different peers every day. One day, a student may be the more knowledgeable other in the Zone of Proximal Development (Vygotsky, 1978) and will provide scaffolding for the less knowledgeable students in the group. The next day that student may be the less knowledgeable member of the group and have to articulate to the other group members what is unclear or difficult about the particular problem. This challenges the more knowledgeable group members to articulate their knowledge clearly, helping them identify gaps in their own understanding and enhancing their learning.

Since our primary goal was to prepare students to use computers for problem solving in a variety of domains, we decided that problem-based learning had to be a major component of the instructional design. We wanted students to use computers to actively solve problems rather than passively listening to lectures. Hence, all instruction takes place in computer laboratories so students are working with computers continuously during class time. Each class consists of a series of focal problems, the solution of which requires students to learn and practice new skills. Each problem builds on previous skills and concepts, extending the range of the students' capabilities (see Figure 5.1).

Institutional demand for the course necessitates an enrollment capacity of 1950 students per semester. The design goal of meeting each class in a computer laboratory coupled with the capacity of the computer laboratories required 65 sections of 30 students. Each section meets twice per week for one hour and 50 minutes per meeting. Resource constraints dictated that each section would be met by teaching assistants (TAs) rather than faculty. Each section has a "lead TA," usually a graduate student, and an "assistant TA," usually an undergraduate student. To ensure instructional consistency across sections, the faculty create detailed lesson plans, exercises and homework assignments for each day's instruction.

Each exercise begins with the lead teaching assistant explaining the problem and leading a discussion about how the concepts apply to the problem. The students next work for 5 to 30 minutes to solve the problem. During this time, the teaching assistants circulate among the students to facilitate the students' work and encourage metacognition about the principles and concepts the problem solving requires. After the students complete each exercise, the lead TA conducts a discussion of the problem, calling on students to review their solutions and asking questions to help the students to reflect on the relative merits of their solutions.

Performance-Based Assessment

Assessment is a critical component of the instructional design. Because we used a collaborative learning model, the assessments needed to be criterion-referenced, rather than norm-referenced. Otherwise, students would view each other as competitors, undermining the goals of collaborative learning (Johnson, Johnson, & Smith, 1991). Since we wanted to evaluate students' problem solving skills, we elected to use performance-based assessments, rather than surrogate measures such as multiple-choice tests.

To accommodate individual student differences, keep assessments consistent with the goals of encouraging student problem solving, and work within the university constraints of a fixed-credit semester, we created modified-mastery, performance-based assessments that we call *Bridge Tasks* (BT).[2] The BTs are authentic assessments in that students use their homework, in-class assignments, textbooks and other instructional materials during bridge tasks to solve a variety of problems representative of those they will have to solve in their majors (Urban-Lurain & Weinshank, 1999b).

Each bridge task is composed of some number of *dimensions* with each dimension containing multiple *instances*. An *instance* is the smallest unit of text that can define a problem, subproblem or a task that is representative of that *dimension*. For example, one dimension may address using reference tools. Within that dimension, there are several instances. One instance may require the students to use a thesaurus to look up a synonym for a particular word. Another may ask students to use the dictionary to insert a definition of a word into a document. The next dimension may address text fonts, with one instance of 10-point Times Roman, another of 12-point Helvetica, and so on.

Each bridge task is constructed by randomly selecting a single instance from each dimension and combining them so that each student receives a unique bridge task. The bridge task appears to the student as a long "story problem" in which the student has realistic scenarios of problems to solve. The creation, maintenance, delivery and record keeping needed to address these factors require an elaborate, database-driven software infrastructure (Urban-Lurain & Weinshank, 1999a).

To test transfer, each bridge task contains one or more *extension tasks* on which students must apply the concepts and principles they have learned to solve new problems they have not previously encountered. Although learning a set of skills for using particular software may allow students to complete routine parts of the BTs, they must be able to apply the underlying concepts or principles to complete the extension tasks.

Bridge tasks are evaluated on a mastery pass/fail basis. If a student demonstrates mastery on the first bridge task, she or he passes the BT and "locks in" a grade of 1.0 in the course. If a student fails a bridge task, she or he must repeat the failed bridge task until passing before taking the next bridge task. Each time a student repeats a BT, she or he receives different instances of each dimension, so the repeated BT tests the same concepts but with different specific problems. For each additional bridge task passed, the student's course grade is incremented by 0.5 until she or he has passed the 3.0 bridge task. Once students pass the 3.0 bridge task, they may earn a 3.5 or 4.0 by completing a semester project to demonstrate their ability to integrate the concepts and competencies they have mastered throughout the course.

In traditional mastery learning, students continue to work on the course materials until they demonstrate mastery of specified materials at the desired level. They do not take a fixed set of examinations in order to receive a grade on the basis of single-attempt assessments (Block, Efthim, & Burns, 1989; Levine, 1985). However, at Michigan State University, students are expected to complete courses within a single semester, so we used a *modified*-mastery model. Students have a maximum of twelve opportunities to take bridge tasks during the semester; there are a total of five bridge tasks that students must pass to be eligible to complete the final project. Thus, students may take each bridge task two times and still be able to complete them all by the end of the semester. For students who have not passed the 3.0 BT at the end of the semester, their final course grade is the highest BT they have passed at that time.

Khattri, Reeve, and Kane (1998) classify performance assessments into two broad categories. Task-centered performance assessments evaluate particular skills and competencies using clear-cut scoring rubrics. Construct-centered performance assessments emphasize general skills, but do not have clear-cut scoring guidelines and are more difficult to use for summative evaluation. Bridge tasks fall into the task-centered category, allowing for detailed scoring rubrics to ensure high inter-rater reliability. The BT database contains the scoring rubrics used by the raters to evaluate the students' performance on the BTs. The granularity of the scoring rubrics allows us to create sophisticated, problem-based, performance assessments on a large scale (more than 14,000 BTs per semester) with scoring rubrics that produce grading error rates of less than 5%.

Inter-task reliability is another concern with a large number of complex performance measurements (Raymond & Viswesvaran, 1993). Student performance can be affected by variability in the sampling of the particular tasks that they receive. The granularity of the bridge task dimensions allows for analysis of the variability of each instance within the dimensions. We use these analyses to revise the instances to reduce the variance within each dimension of the BTs. Because students have up to twelve opportunities to take BTs, their grades are not dependent upon a particular instance of a BT. These two factors mean that the BTs have high generalizability (Shavelson, Baxter, & Gao, 1993).

There are several advantages to this assessment model. First, bridge tasks are criterion-referenced, not norm-referenced. Although students complete the bridge tasks individually, they are not evaluated on a competitive basis; students' grades are not dependent on doing better or worse than their peers. Second, bridge tasks provide formative feedback, resulting in a greater opportunity for learning than traditional multiple-choice examinations. The students' motivation shifts from accumulating points to mastering the concepts so they can complete tasks similar to those they will encounter in their subsequent courses and after graduation. Third, bridge tasks provide summative feedback; the course grade actually indicates which concepts and competencies a student has mastered. In courses that use norm-referenced assessment, a grade of 2.0 often means that a student has accumulated the average number of points from a variety of exams and homework assignments. The grade does not indicate what knowledge the student does or does not have. In this model, the course grade reflects the concepts and competencies on which a student has demonstrated mastery.

EVALUATION OF THE STUDENTS' CONCEPTUAL UNDERSTANDING

The size of the student population and the granularity of the assessments provide a rich data set that allow us to model the students' conceptual frameworks and understand how the BT skills and concepts measure FIT-ness. Briefly, we use discriminant analysis to predict student performance using BT dimensions as the predictor variables. To understand the structural relationships among the individual BT dimensions, we examine the correlations between the variables and the rotated functions. Table 5.1 shows these correlations based on more than 5000 students who took the course over three semesters. For a more extensive discussion of the analytic procedures see Urban-Lurain (2000).

We can "view" the correlations in Table 5.1 either along the rows or down the columns. If we look across the rows, we can see on which function, or functions, each variable loads most strongly, indicating how the skills measured by each variable are organized in the students' minds. Some variables load primarily on a single function. For example, *Computer specifications* correlates primarily with function 6 ($r = .859$) but does not

Table 5.1.   Correlations Between Variables and Rotated Functions

Variable	1	2	3	4	5	6	7
Boolean Search	.067	.013	.443^	.489*	−.097	−.094	.332
Create Excel chart	.637*	−.076	.099	.004	−.018	.106^	−.005
Computer specifications	.205^	.145	−.070	.159	.006	.859*	.011
Create private folder	.200^	.893*	−.154	.164	−.087	.032	.032
Find and rename file	.033	.006	.170	.012	.269	.345^	.395*
Excel function	.783*	−.041	.036	−.249^	−.020	−.035	−.060
Find new application	.054	−.011	.090	−.003	.812*	.033	.101^
Footnotes in Word	.287^	.536*	−.251	.264	.193	−.132	.116
Modify styles in Word	.253	.342^	−.369*	.307	.340	.140	.296
New spreadsheet	.727*	−.139	.193^	.028	−.061	.016	−.029
Own web page URL	−.019	.070	.307^	.710*	.045	.007	−.075
Table of contents	.230	.291	−.085	.400^	.224	.173	−.511*
Update spreadsheet	.487*	−.193	.291^	.091	−.183	.032	.188
Web page text formatting	−.020	.418^	.726*	−.152	.214	.030	−.001
Web pages in web folder	−.052	.324^	.797*	−.017	.237	−.021	.004

* Function with which this variable has the largest correlation
^ Function with which this variable has the second largest correlation

have any correlations $r > .205$ on other functions. This indicates that the concepts measured by the *Computer specifications* dimension (computer memory, secondary storage and their relationship to software specifications) are not strongly related to any other concepts in the students' minds. Other variables load moderately on multiple functions. *Modify styles in Word* loads somewhat on all seven of the functions with strength of the correlations ranging from $r = .140$ on function 6 to $r = -.369$ on function 3.

This indicates that students' conceptual understanding associated with the dimension *Modify styles in Word* are more diffuse. Modifying styles requires understanding styles as collections of formatting commands, what the formatting commands impact (character or paragraph attributes), when it is appropriate to modify styles rather than create new ones, and the abstraction of using styles rather than directly applying the formatting to particular sections of text.

By examining the columns in Table 5.1, we gain some insight into the students' conceptual grouping of the BT dimensions. Function 1 loads primarily on the concepts needed to solve more complex spreadsheet problems, as the largest correlations are with the extension task of using new *Excel functions* and the ability to create a *New spreadsheet* that solves a particular problem. Function 2 correlates most strongly with the dimension *Create private folder*, which requires understanding hierarchical networked file systems and the concepts of file permissions in order to create folders that are not accessible by other users. Function 3 correlates primarily with the HTML concepts needed to control *Web page text formatting* and understanding how web servers access files as measured by the dimension *Web pages in web folder*.

DISCUSSION

Recall that Figure 5.1 represents the course's inductive approach to developing conceptual understanding with information technology. As students work on problems that epitomize various computing concepts, their mental schemas triangulate on the concepts. The concept map in Figure 5.2 represents the students' schemas and conceptual frameworks as measured by the function loadings in Table 5.1.

Figure 5.2 is a two-dimensional depiction of the relationships among what are actually seven-dimensional ellipsoids. The volumes, shapes, and locations of these ellipsoids in seven-dimensional space are defined by the seven discriminant functions.

Each of the skills and competencies shown in the figure correlates—to various degrees—with each of the seven discriminant functions. However, to represent this mapping in two dimensions, each of the skills and con-

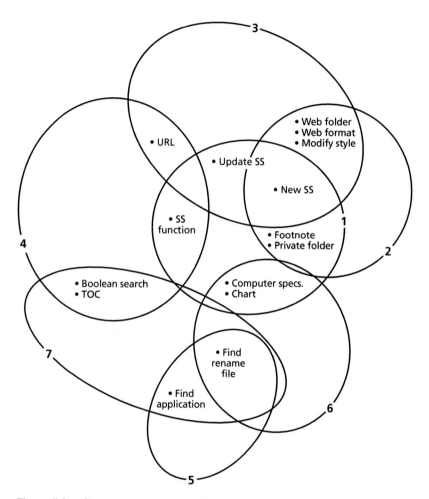

Figure 5.2.   Concept map of computing skill schematic structure.

cepts is located in the intersections of the ellipses representing the two or three functions with which it most strongly correlates. For example, the BT dimensions for *Footnotes,* and *Creating a private folder* are each most strongly correlated with functions 1 and 2. As shown in Table 5.1, the dimension for *Footnotes* also has moderate correlations with functions 4 and 5, but these higher dimensional intersections cannot be represented in two dimensions. The BT dimension *New spreadsheet* correlates primarily with function 1 and—to a lesser degree—with functions 3 and 2. Function 1 is central in this model because seven of the 15 BT dimensions have their top two correlations with this function, accounting for 56.4% of the variance in the model. The concepts of data representation and abstraction underlie the BT dimensions that correlate primarily with this function, indicating that students have correctly clustered these in their schemas of the computing systems.

Each ellipse represents the clustering of different schemas (see Figure 5.1) across the student population. The intersection and clustering of the ellipses represent the way the students' schemas intersect and triangulate on the underlying computing concepts. The actual schematic structure captured by the discriminant functions is too complex to display on this two-dimensional graph. However, the two-dimensional concept map does give a sense of the clustering of the schematic structure. The closer that a skill or competency lies to the middle of the graph, the more abstract and interrelated with other concepts it is in the students' minds. For example, *Find and rename file* and *Find application* both require knowledge of hierarchical file systems and appear near the outside of the graph. *Private folder* also requires knowledge of hierarchical file systems plus knowledge of networked file system permissions and is clustered with the concepts of data representation abstractions that are necessary to create footnotes, modify styles and control web page formatting.

Several spreadsheet concepts also cluster together. Updating a spreadsheet is conceptually easier than creating a new spreadsheet. Updating primarily requires an understanding of the syntax of spreadsheet formulas. However, creating a new spreadsheet is more complex. It requires the ability to analyze a problem, determine the correct formulas to solve the problem and implement the solution by using the correct spreadsheet syntax.

IMPLICATIONS

We have shown that it is possible to teach FITness without teaching programming. However, the instruction must be based upon an analysis of the critical computing concepts, their interrelationships, and the types of problems that epitomize these concepts at each stage of the learning process. For an inductive approach to work the concepts need to be the right "depth" in relationship to the problems, about one "level" lower than the scope of the problem students are trying to solve. For example, logical operators are a critical computing concept that can be taught at many conceptual levels. One level is that taken in many introductory deductive logic classes, teaching truth-functional composition, consistency trees and derivations. Another level is teaching programming and the use of bitwise operators. Some courses go even lower, teaching about the implementation of logic gates in hardware (e.g., Biermann, Fahmy, Guinn, Pennock, Ramm, & Wu, 1994). Although these are all valid representations of logical operations, knowledge of VLSI circuitry or truth tables is not what is important when trying to locate appropriate information in a vast sea of electronic databases. Translating a vague question into the appropriate set of keywords, combining the keywords with Boolean operators, evaluating the quality of results returned by the search and refining it to locate the relevant information help the learner build an understanding of logical concepts that will meet the needs of FITness.

A Single Computing Course or Computing Across the Curriculum?

One of the goals of FITness is to prepare teachers to use information technology in all facets of their lives. This means that teachers will need to use computing technology as an integral part of their other courses, much as they use writing in many courses. As with teaching writing fluency, there is a debate about teaching FITness in a single course versus "computing across the curriculum." As with the writing debate, there are arguments for and against each perspective.

Computing across the curriculum has several advantages. First, it is contextualized, that is the students learn how computing is used in a particular context while studying that discipline. This improves student motivation, which should enhance retention. On the other hand, there are several pragmatic disadvantages to this approach. As we have seen, FITness requires conceptual understanding. If computing across the curriculum is going to develop that knowledge of computing concepts, the computing aspects of the instruction must be designed to facilitate that conceptual understanding. This means that faculty who develop courses which integrate computing into the curriculum must have a deep conceptual understanding of computing, much deeper than is required for a teacher to be FIT. Given that discipline-specific courses have as their primary focus the discipline content, it seems unlikely that faculty across disciplines are going to have the time or conceptual knowledge of computing to design instruction that effectively builds understanding of the computing concepts.

The advantages and disadvantages of a single computing course are the inverse of "computing across the curriculum." A single course can develop the material in depth and focus on teaching FITness as the primary task. It can provide uniform content so that all students have the same foundation as they arrive in their subsequent courses. Because of the broad demand for FITness, a single course may have a high enrollment demand, so economies of scale can reduce costs. On the other hand, there are many disadvantages to this approach. Foremost is that a single course isolates FITness from the other curriculum in the minds of the faculty who teach the course, the students who take the course and the faculty in other domains.

Faculty who teach these courses often develop them in isolation from the other curriculum, deciding what they think is appropriate to teach without knowledge of how students will use computing in their subsequent courses (Urban-Lurain & Weinshank, 2000). Faculty in other domains may not feel the need to integrate information technology into their courses because the students "had" a computing course. Many students see such a course simply as a requirement—a hurdle to clear—with negative impact on their motivation. Finally, if students do not have opportunities to immediately and continuously to apply what they learn in the computing course in other courses, retention suffers.

There are two solutions to this dilemma. For institutions that chose to approach FITness with a single course, it is important that CS faculty and faculty from other disciplines cooperate on the course design. They must determine the contexts in which computing is used in the various disciplines to provide exemplar problems from the disciplines that highlight the relevant computing concepts. Doing so will produce a course in which the students solve problems that are situated in different domains but epitomize the underlying computing concepts. Crucial to this approach is the cooperation between the CS and other discipline faculties to ensure that the course's problems are relevant to the domains and that the subsequent discipline courses build upon the problems and concepts from the course.

For institutions that prefer to implement computing across the curriculum, the same principles can apply. In this context, the discipline faculty can provide problems within the discipline and their typical solutions. It is important that the discipline faculty treat computing as an important part of the curriculum, not simply as a "tool" to be used to accomplish an end. The CS faculty can work with the discipline faculty to design instruction that highlights the computing concepts and demonstrates using these concepts to solve the problems. This approach will require allocating sufficient time to the computing aspects of the curriculum so that students are able to learn the underlying computing concepts.

Based on our experience in a large university, we believe that the most viable solution for large institutions is to have students take an introductory course that provides the foundations by focusing on the computing concepts. Subsequent courses in each discipline should continue to build upon this foundation by integrating computing into course in an authentic manner where students use the information technology to solve problems within their domains that they could not solve without the technology.

CONCLUSION

Some argue that it is not going to be necessary to continue to teach FIT-ness because, as computers become ubiquitous, students will arrive at college already FIT. This argument goes back to the 1980s (e.g., Parker & Schneider, 1987). However, we have found that students are not arriving at our course any more FIT than they did in the 1980s. Students have a great deal of exposure to using computers, but have little conceptual understanding when they come into our course. As a result, they have little ability to apply technology to the solution of new problems in ways that technology uniquely enables.

One reason that we cannot assume that students will arrive from high school FIT is because FITness is contextual. FITness for K–12 students is not necessarily sufficient for college students. Students need to use computing technology to solve problems in domains that they are studying in college and will need instruction that focuses on problems that are typical of those they will encounter in their college courses. Furthermore, FITness requires conceptual understanding that will not result from superficial training on particular features of applications software. Teaching for FIT-ness must focus on problem solving, with an emphasis on transfer, so students will be able to keep abreast of rapidly evolving technology and use it to solve new problems in new ways.

The impact and use of computing technology—and the definition of FITness—evolves differently across disciplines. Today, disciplines that had not previously used computers are continuously finding new ways to use them. A few years ago, "innovative" teachers used computers for administrative tasks, such as tracking student grades in a spreadsheet. Now, computing is infusing all areas of the K–12 curriculum. Therefore, teachers must understand computing concepts well enough to be able to find innovative ways of helping students learn with—and about—these technologies, across all disciplines, to prepare students for a lifetime of FITness.

NOTES

1. The Michigan State University design team consisted of Don Weinshank, Professor, Department of Computer Science and Engineering; Mark Urban-Lurain, Instructor, Department of Computer Science and Engineering; Gary McCuaig, Instructional Designer/Producer, Instructional Television; Ryan McFall, Ph.D. candidate, Department of Computer Science and Engineering; and Tom Danieli, M.S. candidate, Department of Computer Science and Engineering.

2. We coined the term *Bridge Task* to convey many different ideas. First, students are concerned about how their grades are determined and bring years

of experience and expectations about assessments to the course. Bridge tasks are not regular norm-referenced "tests" with which most students are familiar; they are different than any assessments they have previously experienced. A unique term helps break the students' preconceptions. Second, the assessments test transfer. Students must use the material from the class and their conceptual understanding as a "bridge" to solving new problems. Third, the assessments are based on a mastery model. Students must cross each "bridge" in the sequence before coming to the next "bridge." Finally— following on the physical bridge metaphor—some students have a hard time changing perspectives on assessments; they are used to collecting "points" as an extrinsic reward. To those students, the instructors can seem to be "trolls under the bridge" (Asbjörnsen & Moe, 1859/1969, pp. 184–185) when they are required to demonstrate mastery by repeating any bridge tasks they do not pass.

REFERENCES

Anderson, R.C. (1984). *The architecture of cognition.* Cambridge, MA: Harvard University Press.

Asbjörnsen, P.C., & Moe, J.I. (1859/1969). The three Billy-goats gruff. In *Popular tales from the Norse* (pp. 184–185). London: The Bodley Head Ltd.

Biermann, A.W., Fahmy, A.F., Guinn, C., Pennock, D., & Wu, P. (1994, March). *Teaching a hierarchial model of computation with animation software in the first course.* Paper presented at the Twenty-Fifth SIGCSE technical symposium on computer science education, Phoenix, AZ.

Block, J.H., Efthim, H.E., & Burns, R.B. (1989). *Building effective mastery learning schools.* New York: Longman.

Bruner, J.S. (1960). *The process of education.* New York: Vintage Books.

Chandler, P., & Sweller, J. (1991). Cognitive load theory and the format of instruction. *Cognition and Instruction, 8*(4), 292–332.

Committee on Information Technology Literacy. (1999). *Being fluent with information technology* (Book and web site NSF Contract Number CDA-9616681). Washington, DC: National Academy of Sciences.

Foshay, R. (1991, May). Sharpen up your schemata. *Data Training,* 18–25.

Johnson, D.W., Johnson, R.T., & Smith, K.A. (1991). *Active learning: Cooperation in the college classroom.* Edina, MN: Interaction Book Company.

Keller, J.M. (1983). Motivational design of instruction. In C.M. Reigeluth (Ed.), *Instructional-design theories and models: An overview of their current status* (pp. 383–434). Hillsdale, NJ: Lawrence Erlbaum Associates.

Khattri, N., Reeve, A.L., & Kane, M.B. (1998). *Principles and practices of performance assessment.* Mahwah, NJ: Lawrence Erlbaum Associates.

Levine, D.U. (1985). *Improving student achievement through mastery learning programs.* San Francisco: Jossey-Bass.

Parker, J.D., & Schnedier, G.M. (1987, February). *Problems with and proposals for service courses in computer science.* Paper presented at the Eighteenth SIGCSE technical symposium on computer science education, St. Louis, MO.

Raymond, M.R., & Viswesvaran, C. (1993). Least squares models to correct for rater effects in performance assessment. *Journal of Educational Measurement, 30*(3), 253–368.

Reigeluth, C.M., & Stein, F.S. (1983). The elaboration theory of instruction. In C.M. Reigeluth (Ed.), *Instruction-design theories and models: An overview of their current status* (pp. 338–381). Hillsdale, NJ: Lawrence Erlbaum Associates.

Rodriguez, R.V., & Anger, F.D. (1981, June). *A novel approach to computer literacy for natural science students.* Paper presented at the National Educational Computing Conference, North Texas State University, Denton.

Shavelson, R.J., Baxter, G.P., & Gao, X. (1993). Sampling variability of performance assessments. *Journal of Educational Measurement, 30*(3), 215–232.

Shuell, T.J. (1986). Cognitive conceptions of learning. *Review of Educational Research, 56*(4), 411–436.

Smith, J.P., III, diSessa, A.A., & Roschelle, J. (1993). Misconceptions reconceived: A constructivist analysis of knowledge in transition. *The Journal of the Learning Sciences, 3*(2), 115–163.

Tu, J.J., & Johnson, J.R. (1990). Can computer programming improve problem-solving ability? *SIGCSE Bulletin, 22,* 30–33, 37.

Urban-Lurain, M. (2000). *Teaching for fluency with information technology: An evaluative study.* Unpublished Ph.D. dissertation, Michigan State University, East Lansing.

Urban-Lurain, M., & Weinshank, D. (1999a). "I do and I understand:" Mastery model learning for a large non-major course. *Special Interest Group on Computer Science Education, 30,* 150–154.

Urban-Lurain, M., & Weinshank, D. (1999b, April). *Mastering computer technology: A new approach for non-computer science majors.* Paper presented at the AERA Annual Meeting, Montreal.

Urban-Lurain, M., & Weinshank, D. (2000, October). *Is there a role for programming in non-major CS courses?* Paper presented at the Frontiers in Education 2000 conference, Kansas City, MO.

Urban-Lurain, M., & Weinshank, D. (2001). Do non-computer science students need to program? *Journal of Engineering Education, 90*(4), 535–541.

Vygotsky, L. (1978). *Mind in society: The development of higher psychological processes.* Cambridge, MA: Harvard University Press.

Weinshank, D.J., Urban-Lurain, M., Danieli, T., & McCuaig, G. (1992). *Integrated introduction to computing.* Dubuque, IA: Kendall/Hunt Publishing Company.

Weinshank, D.J., Urban-Lurain, M., Danieli, T., & McCuaig, G. (1995). *Integrated introductin to computing* (rev. & enlarged ed.). Dubuque, IA: Kendall/Hunt Publishing Company.

Yelon, S.L. (1996). *Powerful principles of instruction.* White Plains, NY: Longman.

CHAPTER 6

TECHNOLOGY-SUPPORTED PORTFOLIO PROCESSES DESIGNED TO PROMOTE LEARNING IN A TEACHER PREPARATION PROGRAM

Cheryl L. Rosaen and Tom Bird

MAKING TECHNOLOGY DO REAL WORK IN TEACHER PREPARATION

Like many teacher educators, we face dramatically increased expectations for the quality of preparation of new teachers (Interstate New Teacher Assessment and Support Consortium [INTASC], 1992; National Commission on Teaching and America's Future [NCTA], 1996). These expectations include preparing teacher candidates to use information technologies as professional and pedagogical tools (International Society for Technology in Education [ISTE], 1999; NCATE, 1997). When our teacher preparation program adopted technology requirements several years ago, our faculty decided to infuse work toward those requirements into existing courses, instead of offering a separate course, so that informa-

What Should Teachers Know About Technology?: Perspectives and Practices, pages 75–98
Copyright © 2003 by Information Age Publishing
All rights of reproduction in any form reserved.

tion technology could be linked with the substance of our program (Gill-ingham & Topper, 1999). We agreed with that approach. Pressed for time in an ambitious curriculum, we also held that the technology should do real work in our courses, both because there was very much work to be done, and because authentic uses promise more useful and meaningful learning of the technology (Reeves, 1996). In short, while we intend that teacher candidates should learn a good deal about educational uses of information technology, we have treated that technology entirely as a tool or medium, as distinct from a content, of our courses.

For us, the aim of making technology do the real work of our courses immediately brought two matters to the fore. First, before prospective teachers enter teacher preparation, they have already formed many habits of mind regarding teaching and learning; we also know that these habits tend to persist throughout a teacher preparation program (Anderson & Bird, 1995; Lortie, 1975; Wideen, Mayer-Smith, & Moon 1998). At the same time, teacher candidates have formed habits of course-taking that often lead them to produce what is asked in each course, sell the books, shelve or trash the notes, and move on. On their own, it seems, few teacher candi-dates habitually make connections across courses and field experiences. Such fragmented work in a teacher preparation program is unlikely to exert much influence on teacher candidates' experiences and strongly held ideas. Our faculty had been working to make our program more coherent and continuous in order to increase its effect; we wondered whether information technology could stimulate and support a parallel effort by teacher candidates themselves to learn in more coherent and powerful ways.

Second, we aim to promote a range of professional processes and habits that are likely to enable teacher candidates to engage in goal-directed learning throughout their teaching careers. Those habits and processes include disciplined curiosity about teaching, learning, and their contexts; engagement in thoughtful goal setting; deliberate acquisition and deliber-ative application of knowledge and skills; generating and demonstrating new knowledge with colleagues; and taking responsibility for self-assess-ment. Like others, we have been asking whether those *professional* processes and habits can be achieved partly through *portfolio* processes and habits, and whether information technology can support the latter.

Across the many efforts to foster and represent professional learning of novice and experienced teachers with teaching portfolios (Cambridge, 2001; Georgi & Crowe, 1998; Johnson, 1999; McKinney, 1998; McLaughlin & Vogt, 1996; McLaughlin, Vogt, Anderson, Du Mez, Peter, & Hunter, 1998; Wigle & White, 1998; Wilcox & Tomei, 1999), there is considerable variation in the purposes of portfolios (e.g., learning, assessment, employ-ment); their audiences; and their structure, content, and processes (Wolf

& Dietz, 1998). Many teacher educators have documented portfolios' strong potential in fostering professional reflection and learning; however, the use of portfolios is complex, labor intensive, and developmentally demanding for both faculty and teacher candidates (Winsor, Butt, & Reeves, 1999). While we are optimistic that teaching portfolios might help us to address the issues of coherence and continuity in our teacher preparation program, we also see come complex issues: *How can professional portfolios become integrated and embedded within and across program courses to increase the likelihood that they will become a meaningful professional learning tool, and not just another assignment or project to complete? What role could technology play in supporting portfolio processes that foster professional learning? How might the demands of the technology complicate the matter?* We hold that the design and implementation of any program innovation must be integrally connected to the program's curriculum, instruction and assessment practices. With support from our college's Preparing Tomorrow's Teachers to Use Technology (PT3) grant from the Department of Education, we have been pursuing those questions.

In the course of our work, we formed a conception of professional development and portfolio processes that drew heavily on Wilcox and Tomei's (1999) *Professional Portfolios for Teachers* and on some of our own work (Bird, 1990; Rosaen, 2001). In our discussions, a professional portfolio is constantly constructed and reconstructed across the career in support of four *professional development processes:* (a) "*collecting*" tools and materials for teaching; (b) "*working*" with those tools and materials in professionally educative ways, (c) "*sharing*" those tools and materials with colleagues in professional conversation, and (d) "*showcasing*" elements of one's practice to colleagues, assessors, potential employers, or certification boards. In the first two processes, the portfolio functions as a *workspace* for the prospective teacher. In the third and fourth processes, the portfolio or some annotated selection from the portfolio, functions as a *display* for conversation with colleagues or for assessment processes.

To make information technology do real work in portfolio processes, we must learn how teacher candidates engage (or do not engage), construe (or misconstrue), and respond (or mis-respond) to the course assignments and to the software and other technological tools used to execute them. Like others who engage in action research, we are planning several cycles of inquiry (Elliott, 1991; Oja & Smulyan, 1989) to inform our building of technology-supported portfolio processes from the ground up, so that they are an integral part of the program's curriculum, teaching, and assessment practices.

In the first section of this chapter, we will outline the course requirements and software we designed for two pre-internship courses to engage teacher candidates in technology-supported portfolio processes and describe our study of the use of those processes.[1] Then we will report our initial findings regarding student perceptions of their initial and developing technology skills and uses, their perceptions and assessments of technology-supported portfolio processes, and their engagement in those processes. In closing, we will discuss how technology-supported tasks and assignments might serve as "boundary objects" (Wenger, 1998) that enable teacher candidates to make connections within and across courses, and so to achieve coherence in their programs. We speculate on how we might design future course requirements.

CRAFTING COURSE REQUIREMENTS AS TECHNOLOGY-SUPPORTED PORTFOLIO PROCESSES

We have taken two different approaches to our use of technology in support of the four portfolio processes. The brief sketch provided here will be followed by more details later in the chapter. In both courses, teacher candidates were issued laptop computers (unless they preferred to use their own computers) that were equipped with appropriate software for completing assigned projects. In TE 301, Tom Bird took a direct and uniform approach that asked all teacher candidates in his section to use one specific piece of software, TeachersFile, to work with course content in four course assignments.[2] Teacher candidates began using the software by writing and explaining five to ten goals they currently held as teachers; they then made records of and labels for those ideas in TeachersFile. As they conducted two inquiries into teaching and learning, they were asked to employ ideas and options collected in their TeachersFiles. In a 30-minute session with each teacher candidate during the last three weeks of the course, Tom posed teaching situations that called for knowledge of options likely to have been encountered in the course. He asked each candidate what she or he could find in the File that would help to interpret and act in the situation, and offered advice about the File as she or he then saw it. In TE 301, then, all of the teacher candidates were required to use one piece of software that was built to support the collecting and working portfolio processes, and that provided tools for excerpting, summarizing, labeling, sorting, linking, and finding.

In TE 401, Cheryl Rosaen used an indirect approach that embedded multiple opportunities—a menu of options—for teacher candidates to choose to use technology (or not), with support, as a cognitive and communication tool as they completed an array of assignments across the semester. The assignments included creating an organizational framework for a teacher resource file; planning and teaching lessons; and using and appraising assessment tools and educational software in the classroom. Teacher candidates were taught to use PowerPoint and the basics of creating a web page, and spent some class time exploring web sites and learning to create bookmarks. An end-of-course *Philosophy Statement* could be written in narrative, essay, or hypermedia form (e.g., web site with artifacts, photos, written commentary). Multiple examples of ways to use technology in support of these assignments were shared, and support outside of class in using technology was available.

Studying Issues of Interaction and Engagement

The two pilot tests share a conceptual and practical issue. Teacher candidates' continuous experience shapes their construal of and co-construction of the course with the instructor, with more or less favorable influences on the habits of mind they will carry into teaching (Dewey, 1938). Concerning these interactions, we are compelled to investigate the extent to which teacher candidates engaged with the content and activities of the course in meaningful ways. One challenge we face is how teacher candidates conceptualize learning to teach, and whether they believe that a teacher preparation program has anything to offer them (Calderhead, 1991). We have worked steadily to craft tasks that are arguably authentic for teaching, we made those arguments explicit, and offered options within areas of constrained choice.

One aspect of authenticity we were curious about is whether the teacher candidates perceived the tasks to be connected to the real work of teaching. We have good reason to believe that the teacher candidates will use their minds very differently depending on their goal orientation. In our experience, many of them conceive of taking university courses and becoming a teacher in ways that would lead them to set performance (extrinsic) goals focused on obtaining a grade rather than mastery (intrinsic) goals focused on learning and understanding (Pintrich, Marx, & Boyle, 1993). A second aspect of authenticity we explored is the extent to which teacher candidates developed a sense of ownership of the tasks in pursuit of their own professional goals.

Finally, we must consider the fact that teacher candidates were asked to use computers and networks to do much of the work of each course. As others have already documented, teacher candidates' confidence level, attitudes and beliefs about technology, their responses to challenges, and their own skills and expertise in using technology have the potential to influence what they take away from their experiences (Keiffer, Hale, & Templeton, 1998; Laffey & Musser, 1998; McKinney, 1998; Willis & Mehlinger, 1996; Winsor et al., 1999). We wondered whether the information technology could help candidates to pursue educative tasks that seemed to them to be connected to the real work of teaching and to their own goals for learning.

Research Questions and Design

We investigated the following questions to more clearly understand issues of continuity and interaction, and to learn more about teacher candidates' engagement within the two courses:

- How do the teacher candidates perceive and interpret the software and assignments?
- What do the teacher candidates view as important and authentic about engaging in the portfolio processes?
- What issues, challenges, practical limitations or impediments emerge as they engage in them?
- What are necessary support structures?
- What role does the use of technology play in the portfolio processes?

Regarding these questions, we collected the following data: (a) multiple choice pre- and post-surveys in which teacher candidates assessed their basic skills in technology, (b) a multiple choice pre- and post-survey on the range and frequency of technology uses for TE 401 students, and (c) a brief essay by the candidates concerning their attitudes about technology at the beginning of the course. The essays were reviewed to construct a picture of teacher candidates' attitudes about technology at the beginning of the course. Summaries of survey results were reviewed to document changes in teacher candidates' perceptions of their technology competencies and uses of technology over time.

In addition, in TE 301 Tom collected various course materials: three short in-class writing assignments about how teacher candidates regard their work with the TeachersFile; audio tape of or notes on 30-minute office visits late in the semester to work with TeachersFile, along with a copy of the state of the TeachersFile at the time of the visit; and a copy of the final state of each candidate's File at the end of the semester, along with copies of their papers for the course; instructor plans and course materials.

For TE 401 students, Cheryl collected a variety of data: copies of weekly reflective writing and all written assignments, web addresses for teacher candidates' web pages, instructor plans and course materials, course evaluations, and an end-of-course short-answer survey on laptop uses.

We examined these data to understand how teacher candidates perceived the software and assignments; what they viewed as important about engaging in portfolio processes; what issues, challenges, and impediments emerged; support structures needed; and the role technology played (if any) in the portfolio processes.[3] Following standards for qualitative methodology (Bogdan & Biklen, 1982; Erickson, 1986), we looked for patterns and themes within and across the data and sought disconfirming evidence to test them. Unless noted, assertions made are supported by more than one data source.

ENGAGING TEACHER CANDIDATES
IN PORTFOLIO PROCESSES

Our surveys indicated that, in general, teacher candidates entered the courses willing to work with technology and some were even quite interested in and enthusiastic about the prospect. Generally, technical considerations did not get in the way of professional learning—which is important because our program does not offer a separate course in the use of educational technology. Candidates in TE 301 reported considerably more skill with computer software at the end of the course than at the beginning. Candidates in TE 401 reported both increased skills and modestly increased uses of a range of software. These findings are detailed in a parallel report (Bird & Rosaen, 2001). Without controls, one cannot attribute the growth to the courses, but for our purposes it is sufficient support for the work that growth occurred.

Supposing that the technical aspects of the technology-supported portfolio processes could be managed, our next and main concern was to explore the extent to which teacher candidates engaged substantially in those processes. As explained earlier, we wanted to induce mastery goals that would be likely to promote deep processing, cognitive reorganization, and retention over time. To describe productive engagement for TE 301, we will draw on data describing the candidates' uses of TeachersFile. To describe engagement in TE 401, we will summarize teacher candidates' own assessments of the teacher's portfolio options that they were offered.

How the Teacher Candidates Engaged TeachersFile

TeachersFile's organizing visual metaphor is a set of file folders, each presenting a database record. Each folder can contain as little as a short text in the folder label, along with two keywords chosen from editable menus to support searches of the folders. A given folder can also contain text as well as digitized graphics, photographs, sound, and video. Each folder provides menus for applying several sets of keywords—keyword sets are also provided, but are editable by the user.

Fifteen of the 18 teacher candidates granted permission to analyze their completed TeachersFiles. Combining their contents in a spreadsheet provided means to look for patterns in their use of TeachersFile (see Table 6.1).

Table 6.1. Patterns of use of the options in TeachersFile

	Diane	Eleanor	Erica	Janice	Jasmin	Jessie	Julia	Kate	Kathy	Laura	Lucy	Nancy	Sarah	Sophie	Stevi
Timing and Length of Entries															
1. Weeks used to make 5+ rec'ds	4	2	7	3	7	2	9	4	3	5	5	6	5	7	4
2. % rec'ds made through week 11	4%	3%	34%	2%	16%	0%	58%	34%	3%	9%	7%	28%	50%	77%	36%
3. Total records made	159	187	251	141	190	186	156	185	183	172	137	177	193	184	103
4. Mean number words in Label	8	10	17	7	9	7	8	7	14	11	10	7	11	7	7
5. % rec'ds with both Label and Text	6%	20%	19%	50%	36%	35%	35%	34%	96%	26%	28%	42%	33%	44%	64%
5b. Mean number words in Text	38	21	45	43	21	25	52	32	17	35	38	24	34	28	38
6. Filed inquiry project reports			Both	Both	Both	Both	Both			One	Both		Both	One	
Links Made															
7. % of rec'ds linked to other rec'ds	0%	0%	18%	18%	35%	6%	26%	0%	99%	29%	30%	53%	2%	0%	0%
7b. Mean number of links			1.3	1.6	3.8	4.0	2.2		5.0	2.2	1.6	2.6	1.5		
Editing and Use of Key Words															
8. Goal keywords per record	1.0	1.0	1.4	1.0	1.1	1.0	1.7	1.0	1.3	1.0	1.0	1.1	1.2	1.4	1.0
9. Terms added to Record Type menu	3	0	4	3	1	0	3	2	6	0	2	1	2	3	1
9b. % rec'ds using added terms	36%	0%	47%	16%	1%	0%	7%	7%	22%	0%	2%	6%	15%	35%	4%
10. Terms added to Function menu	8	11	12	6	1	0	3	8	33	3	10	4	7	17	1
10b. % rec'ds using added terms	69%	98%	78%	21%	4%	0%	15%	58%	97%	39%	62%	11%	59%	60%	4%
11. Named a YouNameIt menu	Yes	Yes	Yes		Yes			Yes							
11.b % rec'ds using NameIt menu	0%	0%	4%	0%	54%	0%	9%	13%	0%	0%	0%	10%	0%	0%	0%
12. Times other menus used	4	0	503	0	0	0	167	5	0	0	4	2	7	80	11
Rating the Use of TeachersFile															
13. Tom's total rating of qualities	3.0	3.0	4.0	3.0	3.0	3.0	3.5	3.0	4.0	3.5	3.0	3.5	3.5	3.0	3.0

There were variations in *timing and length of entries*, including when records were made (Table 6.1, lines 1 and 2), the total number of records (line 3), and the lengths and location of text material (lines 4 through 5b). TeachersFile included convenient means to link any record with any other record, so that the user could then move quickly among linked records by clicking buttons. Because these links may indicate candidates' attempts to connect their learning, two types of *links made* were examined: the percentage of records linked to other records (Table 6.1, line 7) and the mean number of links (line 8). TeachersFile provided fourteen keyword menus to label records for sorting and searching, but users could edit any menu's vocabulary to make it entirely their own, so *use of key words* was examined. By design, three menus were most likely to be used. Lines 8 through 10b of Table 6.1 summarize the candidates' editing of those three menus. Two of the fourteen menus could be both edited and named (lines 11 and 11b). Line 12 summarizes the number of times other menus were used.

At the end of the semester, as part of the course grading, Tom *rated the repertoire constructed in each TeachersFile* using an analytic rubric that attended to many of the aspirations for the File and that summed to 1.0 through 4.0. The sums appear in line 13 of Table 6.1. Tom found all of these Files to be better-than-adequate attempts, particularly considering that teacher candidates were working with new, crude, and sometimes balky software. In their visits to Tom's office, all of the candidates could use the sorting and finding options to treat their Files as databases if they cared to. If we consider only these data, which of the teacher candidates might have been engaged in an authentic, mastery-oriented effort to use their Files to engage in the portfolio processes of collecting and working? One must be cautious here; some teacher candidates will go to considerable lengths to contrive whatever product they believe an instructor wants and the instructor can be satisfied. Note that Tom assigned the same rating to Eleanor's late, hasty effort as to Sophie's more systematic and seemingly goal-directed effort. Setting that reservation aside, one might nominate Erica, Janice, Jasmin, Julia, Kate, Kathy, Nancy, Sarah, and Sophie as authentic and deliberate users, because each provides three or more reasons to do so (see the bold print in names and numbers in Table 6.1).

If these candidates were doing more than merely following instructions, what were they doing? They were expressing intentions and aspirations that they already held as teachers, and were adding to or refining their list of intentions as they interacted with the matter of TE 301. Of 286 records labeled as goals, 110 were made after November 30. From the subject matter of the course, they were selecting expressions of ideas and teaching options as having particular significance or attraction for them. Using keyword menus, they were labeling those ideas and options as relevant to one or more of their goals. Primarily by editing and applying another menu, they were classifying the ideas and options they gathered as being of similar kind, and thus available to retrieve together as needed. By way of the linking machinery in the TeachersFile, they were declaring that some of those ideas and options bore particular relations to other ideas and options that they have gathered. Arguably, these data indicate that some of the candidates were using TeachersFile to collect and work with options for thought and action in teaching.

Engagement with the Teacher's Portfolio Processes

To assess TE 401 candidates' engagement with the opportunities they were provided, we examined their ratings in end-of-course evaluations. They were asked to indicate how well they thought *the course* supported their learning to teach language arts and mathematics, in relation to each of five course goals, and to rate each *course assignment.* On a scale where 1 is "least helpful" and 4 is "most helpful," averages of teacher candidates' ratings of the course ranged from 3.5 to 3.7, with an overall average of 3.65. The ratings of course assignments ranged from 2 to 4 and the overall average for all ratings was 3.5. Overall, they found the course and its assignments to be quite supportive of their professional learning.

Narrative comments given with each rating and additional comments made in class are displayed in Table 6.2 below. They illuminate ways in which teacher candidates experienced the assignments and how technology played a role (if any).

Table 6.2.   Teacher Candidates' Comments about Course Assignments

Average Rating	Comments
Educational Software Appraisal 2.98	• appreciated experience of using software–exposure • did not use software on a regular basis in classroom • unsure how that experience will apply to the future
Attendance and Participation (Class & Field Time) 3.6	• appreciated multiple opportunities to collaborate with colleagues, try out ideas, engage in discussions • valued instructors' extensive use of hypermedia databases to see standards-based practices • appreciated exposure to variety of web sites and opportunity to learn about ways to categorize and organize them • liked learning "basics" of developing a web page and viewing samples for future reference, but did not have time to make own • enjoyed making and sharing "All About Me" PowerPoint presentations and sharing with children in classroom (laptops made sharing feasible)

Table 6.2.   Teacher Candidates' Comments about Course Assignments

Average Rating	Comments
	• 12 teacher candidates worked with technology in the classroom (e.g., used computer to write letters to parents, made materials for classroom use, used scanner and digital camera, accessed internet as part of instruction, used laptop to tutor ESL student, developed a class web page, developed electronic portfolios)
Resource File Framework 3.6	• appreciated setting up an organizational system early in their professional preparation • appreciated seeing others' frameworks for additional ideas • 1 teacher candidate stored her web sites on a disk • 1 teacher candidate developed her own web page which included categorized web site links • 5 teacher candidates mentioned "getting started" on a web page as a complement to their physical resource file
Philosophy Statements Draft: 3.5 Final: 3.6	• use of laptops for drafting and revising • use of laptops for peer conferencing during drafting processes • 1 teacher candidate used web page to "showcase" final Philosophy Statement • 1 teacher candidate developed final Philosophy Statement in hypermedia form using PowerPoint • 15 teacher candidates discussed ways they would use technology in the classroom in their final Philosophy Statement (e.g., access software to practice skills and concepts, publishing tool, classroom web page to publish stories and conjectures, sources of information, data bases)
Assessment Tools 3.2	• assignment unnecessary because teacher candidate already engaged in assessment on an ongoing basis • appreciated exposure, but wanted more integration with ongoing classroom participation • 2 teacher candidates worked with children to develop electronic portfolios
Language Arts and Math Lesson and Reflections 4.0	• felt like a "real" teacher • post-lesson analysis of tape recorded discussion helped gain insights about their own teaching and student participation and learning • most teacher candidates used laptops to develop plans, revise and improve them • many accessed internet for lesson ideas, to download pictures and clips as teaching resources, create overheads and assignments

The teacher candidates' ratings and comments suggest that the course assignments satisfied their idea of learning from experience and corresponding emphasis on their time in school classrooms, and thus were helpful in engaging the teacher candidates with the course content.

In general, the provision of multiple options for using technology, to foster their own learning and to learn about the potential of technology for classroom use, seemed comfortable for teacher candidates, and apparently provided authentic contexts for modest increases in their technology skills and uses. Rather than getting in the way of their learning, this approach enabled all teacher candidates to have some degree of experience and success with a range of technology uses, although those experiences varied considerably. Moreover, it appears that teacher candidates used technology more frequently when there was a natural fit with the classroom events, with their own goals for learning technology, with the nature of the assignment, or some combination thereof.

Thus, we see that TE 301 required extensive engagement with one piece of software intended to support collecting and working with options for thought and action. It highly prescribed the software and project genres, but left considerable choice of goals to express, issues to address, information to collect, interpretations to consider, and conclusions to draw. By contrast, TE 401 offered a range of voluntary possibilities for using information technology to undertake chosen work. In both classes, we found appreciable signs that *many* teacher candidates addressed their assignments and options willingly, with some intentions of their own. In addition, a few of the teacher candidates used some information technology in even more substantial ways. We are inclined to say that, for a first try, teacher candidates' engagement in these portfolio processes was satisfactory.

At the same time, the obvious variability in teacher candidates' engagements with our assignments raises the question how to gain ground from here. Looking more closely at some of the "high end" work done by four of the teacher candidates may help to answer that question.

WHAT "HIGH END" USERS WERE DOING

One strong pattern in the survey data regarding basic skills was the gain in self-reported skill from beginning to end of the semester. In TE 301, two of the teacher candidates stand out because their self-ratings of skills at the outset were among the lowest in the class but much higher at the end of the course, and because they turned in the two TeachersFiles to which Tom assigned the highest ratings at the end of the semester.[4] We will not describe the Files' contents here, but will focus on the candidates' use of the File's affordances.

Erica (TE 301): Grasping the use of a Database

In the initial survey of skills, Erica gave herself one of the lowest ratings in the class. In her initial writing about using computers, Erica revealed both her anxiety and that she was enrolled in a three-credit computer science course described as teaching students to understand computing as a user, and to use common software including e-mail clients, web tools, word processors and presentation software, and data handling software. So, Erica might be regarded partly as a case of what could be achieved with high support for technical learning.

When candidates showed Tom their Files near the end of the semester, most of them worked mostly with the *List* view, which showed only the labels of all the folders, as a list, providing a big picture of the collection. Erica, however, worked mostly with the *Connections* view, which showed all of the information and options for one folder at a time. Her comments suggested that she could think of a single record as something like the top card in a stack of cards with identical format, and could navigate among those cards by finding operations, as distinct from the scrolling provided by the List. She said she liked the Connections view because, without changing the view, she could conveniently add *Text* beyond the label, could add keywords from any of the menus, and could make links among the records.

Perhaps her reliance on the Connections view enabled Erica to make far more extensive use of TeacherFile's keyword menus than other teacher candidates. Nine of the 14 menus appear only on that view. Detailed examination of her editing of the keyword menus suggested that grasping several labeling menus as a set of tools for a collection is substantial work, deserving more scaffolding than Tom provided. However, Erica's revision and use of these menus indicates that she is both taking up a set of labeling tools and modifying them to suit her own ideas and purposes.

Erica *linked* 39 of her 251 records; doing so gave her the option of moving quickly among linked records by clicking buttons. Eight of her records were involved in three-way linkages—three ideas about explaining rules, three kinds of routines, or three items about monitoring students during seatwork. One record had five links in a set concerning interaction routines, teaching routines, the teacher getting students' attention, and the students getting the teacher's attention. Since Erica clearly understood that she could gather items by giving them the same keywords and then sorting or finding, it seems that Erica was ensuring that, if she remembered or retrieved any of the items in this set, she would be likely to recollect the others. The set of links helps her to see a set of options for the same situations.

Erica's use of the Connections view for extensive labeling and considerable linking suggests that she had a firm conception of TeachersFile as a database that offered her a range of tools for collecting and working. The high technical support she was receiving in another course might have been essential for that result.

Kathy (TE 301): Making TeachersFile Her Own

Like Erica, Kathy gave herself one of the lowest self-ratings on skill at the beginning of the semester and turned in one of the highest-rated Files at the end. Unlike Erica, Kathy had not taken and was not taking a course using computers; she reported that she had taken a typing class and a word processing class in high school. As the class began work with the File she expressed both anxiety about and enthusiasm for working with technology.

Kathy's File stood apart from others because she used both the shorter *Label* field and the longer Text field in 176 of her 184 records. In 106 of those records, she had used the Text field to enter a cryptic notation of the source from which she drew the material for the record; at her meeting with Tom, she reported that she had noticed that in that way she could make the source appear on the List view of all records. She was making the List view suit her idea of what is useful.

In 70 records, Kathy had gone beyond the Label to elaborate or specify a point. For example, in one record she entered into the folder Label, "hold students accountable: one way of increasing students learning time." In the Text field, she added the slight expansion "communicate assign-ments clearly; monitor students' progress; provide feedback." Kathy was using her own language to explain options offered in the course, showing her construction of meaning as she used the database.

Later in October, Kathy reported that "[TeachersFile] is pretty easy to use. I am having some trouble with links and how to organize them. Also some things are hard to label because I'm not sure what should go where because some things are so specific and some are so broad." Though she claimed at that time to be having some kind of trouble with links, she even-tually used the File's linking machinery to link 99% of her records to some other record, and the mean number of links made per record is 5. Both of these numbers are distant outliers among the teacher candidates in the section (see Table 6.1, lines 7 and 7b). To most of her goals, each of which appeared in one record, Kathy linked as many other records (17) as TeachersFile would allow. It appears that linking became Kathy's main strategy for connecting items in her File.

Kathy's other option for making connections among records had been to apply the same keywords to them and to retrieve them in groups by using the finding or sorting commands. There is a hint why Kathy might have found that strategy less satisfactory. She added far more terms (33) than any other candidate, to the menu for labeling kinds of records. Perhaps the long list of terms grew ungainly and therefore less useful as a means of connecting ideas. Constructing a category system for complex material can be very challenging and Kathy's case raises the question what sort of instruction and scaffolding Tom should have provided for that part of the work.

There were two other small signs that Kathy deliberately made the File her own. Though the one menu already contained the keyword "goal," she changed it to "mygoal," and she used that term to mark all of her goals. Moreover, she alone deleted from her File all eighteen of the records that Tom that had supplied with the File as samples of what might be done. Either by intention or by omission, all other candidates kept all of those records.

Tom's experience in TE 301 is that some teacher candidates are inclined to remain in the role of "good student"; they are able to take assignments intended to provide opportunities for authentic work and turn them into mere contrivances aimed at the highest possible grade. There are signs in both Erica's and Kathy's Files that they have, at least in part, used Teachers-File in authentic projects of collecting their options for thought and action and of working with those options to make them, and the File, their own. Both of their Files were convincing attempts to grasp and organize options for teaching thought and action, in a form that could be carried conveniently into following classes, or into teaching. While Erica's simultaneous enrollment in a computer science class is reason to wonder how much support a teacher candidate might need to use the File most productively, Kathy's similarly low self-rating on skills and similar productivity without a technical course, taken to together with the skill survey results, suggest that the technical demands of the File were manageable by most of the teacher candidates.

TeachersFile as an Introductory Boundary Object

We saw in Erica's and Kathy's uses of TeachersFile that it has the potential to be a powerful tool for collecting and working with key course concepts, proposals, and rules of thumb, in ways that increase and deepen the connections they were able to identify between and among ideas. Because it enables exploration of substantive questions related to course content and makes visible analytic processes, use of TeachersFile provides a context for modeling and scaffolding analytic processes. It also has the potential to engage teacher candidates in goal-oriented learning across the course, which reflects the productive portfolio habits we seek to support teacher candidates in developing. As such, it can become an authentic professional learning tool for engaging in portfolio processes.

We are therefore encouraged to think of use of TeachersFile as an effective *introduction* to using technology as a professional learning tool and as a *boundary object* that can travel with teacher candidates into their senior-year course work, so they can be encouraged to continue using it.[5] We are also inclined to think that by creating more frequent occasions for sharing works-in-progress, we will be able to create occasions for teacher candidates to talk about what they are learning through the use of TeachersFile, to become more aware of the role portfolio processes play in their learning, and to help one another attain uses that are more like those demonstrated by Erica and Kathy. In the past, Tom has found sharing of drafts of assignments to be a productive exercise that shows all of the candidates some of the good work being done in the course. There was little of such sharing of Files in the pilot but since Michigan State University has adopted a new policy requiring all entering freshman to bring personal computers, that option will be increasingly feasible.

Miranda (TE 401): Using Technology for Collecting and Working

Miranda is the only teacher candidate who went beyond the in-class experience of learning to format a web page and make one link. She was eager to try out some of the ideas suggested in class and proposed that she create a web page to earn an "honors option" designation for TE 401, a notation on her transcript that she completed an agreed-upon extra project.

Miranda's web page became a supplement to her Resource File Framework, a workspace for collecting and working with teaching tools and materials. The opening web page contains photos and quotes pertaining to ideas about how children learn. Many of the ideas included there show that Miranda actively made connections between content learned in her course work in the Child Development Program and what she was learning in her Teacher Preparation Program. That page provides links to three main sections.

Her *All About Me* section provides both personal and professional information. She included her resume and her TE 401 Philosophy Statement, and can update these as she continues throughout the program. Each category within the second section, *Web Links*, contains annotations for several web sites and links to those sites, showing that Miranda was moving beyond collecting information to analyze and describe it, and therefore working with materials at a more analytic level. Moving beyond the use of a bookmarking system enabled Miranda to access her web sites from any location, and to build in new categories over time. It also became a place for her to access resources that go beyond the specific content of the course and has the potential to become a rich resource for her experiences *across the program* and beyond.

Her third section, *Technology in the Classroom*, is still under construction. It reflects her goal for second semester, which was to continue her work in her field-placement classroom to develop electronic portfolios. She planned to incorporate an electronic portfolio template that could be used not only with the current classroom but also with her internship classroom and beyond. As with the other sections of her web page, this section can be modified over time as she learns more about classroom uses of portfolios. Thus, she was working with key ideas from the course and using them in multiple contexts.

Miranda began the course with high enthusiasm for learning more about technology and a fairly high level of skill. She rated herself as "expert" in using a word processor and its advanced features, using e-mail and sending attachments, accessing and searching the World Wide Web and creating bookmarks, and six of the eight items relating to working with operating systems. She rated herself as "developing" or "competent" in almost all other areas. The only areas she identified herself as a "novice" were using formulas or functions in a spreadsheet and using a scanner. She reported "no experience" with correcting a locked-up computer, creating a web page, recording an audio file or digitizing a video clip, and creating an electronic presentation. Interestingly, she was given the opportunity to learn to do many of these things either in the course or in her field placement classroom. By the end of the course, she rated herself as at least "developing" in all areas, and an "expert" in 35% of the items. Her average scores for frequency of uses only increased by 4%, indicating that her regular uses of Media for Communication remained stable and uses for Inquiry and Expression did not significantly increase.[6]

Miranda's ratings of the course assignments averaged a 3.5, which shows that overall, she found them quite helpful to her learning, as did the rest of the class (3.4). As for whether the course helped her work toward the stated goals, Miranda's average rating was a 2.9 (lower than the class average of 3.6). She felt the course was less helpful than did most of her peers in helping her learn about a range of strategies and about children as learners. This may be because Miranda is a Child Development major who had already spent a great deal of time in preschool classrooms and her experience thus far in this program (e.g., extensive work in classrooms) had not yet matched what she has come to expect in an education course, and therefore what she might learn from it. Another possibility is that Miranda sets very high goals for herself and therefore held the course to a higher standard than other teacher candidates. A third possibility is that it failed to provide experiences that were as educative as they could have been. Nevertheless, the overall average of a 2.9 is fairly positive.

Miranda made goal-directed use of the menu of opportunities made available in the course to foster her own professional growth. She used technology (e.g., learning to construct a web page) as a tool to foster that growth, and constructed a product that can be refined and used across the remainder of the program and beyond.

Samantha (TE 401): Using Technology for Working and Showcasing

Samantha is the only TE 401 student who elected to create a hypermedia version of her Philosophy Statement instead of writing a paper. She reported that she felt excited about the option of presenting her ideas in another format and wanted to push herself to see what technology would enable her to develop. Thus, she began the course with specific intentions to learn about technology. She incorporated written text, digital photos of her working with an English as a Second Language student in the classroom (she used her laptop in the classroom to work with PowerPoint to assist the student in writing), and video clips discussing her learning across the program. Her reflections on her emerging philosophy reached back to her experiences in her first two teacher education courses and continued on through TE 301 and TE 401, showing that she deliberately tried to make connections across her program experiences, working to analyze and make sense of her own learning over time. This effort went beyond the stated expectations for the assignment, which asked teacher candidates to draw from their *course* experiences to discuss their emerging philosophy in teaching language arts and mathematics. It provided rich illustrations of Samantha's emerging beliefs and factors that shaped those beliefs—both *across the program* and outside the course. Samantha reported that she would like to include this presentation on a web page in the future.

Samantha began the course with enthusiasm for working with technology and she was excited about the prospect of learning more. She rated herself as either "competent" or "expert" on 75% of the items on the Basic Skills Survey. The only areas she reported to have "no experience" with were correcting a locked-up computer and recording an audio file or digitizing a video clip. By the end of the course, she reported herself to be either "competent" or "expert" on 86% of the items, and she learned to digitize video clips as part of creating her Philosophy Statement. Samantha's average rating of course assignments was a 3.7, higher than the overall class average of 3.4. Her average rating of working toward course goals was 3.9, also higher than the class average of 3.6. Apparently, Samantha found the assignments and her work toward course goals to be highly satisfactory for her learning, and technology seemed to play a central role in at least part of that learning.

Miranda and Samantha stood out among the other teacher candidates in TE 401 for their uses of technology in pursuit of their own professional learning goals. Each interpreted and carried out a particular course assignment, using technology, in ways that are authentic to the "real work" of teachers and in the service of personal goals they set for themselves. In each case, technology became a useful tool supporting their professional learning. Their attempts to use technology for their own purposes are interesting examples of teacher candidates engaging in thoughtful goal setting for their professional learning, developing habits of mind that promote that learning, and developing proficiency in using concrete approaches to demonstrate their professional growth. Their work seems closer to our conception of working toward intrinsic, task-involved goals with authentic tasks, and they found ways for technology to serve their own learning goals.

The Teacher's Portfolio as an Integrating Boundary Object

Miranda's and Samantha's goal-oriented uses of technology provided a way for them to synthesize their learning, both within the course and across their course work and other experiences, showing that they were engaged in productive portfolio habits. Their experiences demonstrate the type of coherence across the program, toward which we are working. Miranda's decision to create a web page created an occasion for her to bring together multiple resources from a variety of experiences (web sites, her own writing, classroom-based assessment work) that can be expanded and revised during her internship year and beyond. When Miranda encounters the requirement during her internship year to create a professional portfolio, she already has a "draft template" for doing so, and some potential artifacts to include. The electronic form facilitates revision and easy access. It also provides the option of including video clips of her teaching with commentary.

Similarly, Samantha's decision to map backward to trace her emerging philosophy across her experiences and teacher education courses enabled her to examine consistent themes and issues explored over time and relate those to her current thinking about teaching language arts and mathematics. Her decision to present her ideas in hypermedia form (written text, digital photos, video clips) enabled her to illustrate her ideas more concretely and bring more of herself into her Philosophy Statement. Like Miranda's web page, this Philosophy Statement is a "draft" that can be revised and expanded for inclusion in her professional portfolio. In both cases, the technological skills needed to construct these products has already been developed by the end of the senior year, and therefore is less likely to become a hurdle to overcome during a demanding and busy internship year.

We know that most teacher candidates valued the TE 401 course assignments for their contributions to candidates' learning, but we do not know if they came away with an explicit understanding of portfolio processes per se, or how they might connect their experiences in TE 401 with the construction of a professional portfolio during their internship year.[7] These findings are encouraging us to do more in the future, in terms of structuring and supporting the use of technology in support of the four portfolio processes. For example, the seniors could be required to create a "rough draft" of a portfolio (*collecting* and *working*) with some electronic components (e.g., an electronic component of a teachers resource file, a web-based template for a portfolio which includes a Philosophy Statement) that could be developed further during their second senior-year methods course and throughout their internship year. Their continued use of TeachersFile after TE 301could also become integrated into these efforts. Moreover, we could build in more *sharing* of these products, to raise candidates' awareness of portfolio processes and to expand their visions of what is possible in terms of *showcase* items for the internship year. As it stands now, some teacher candidates did some work with technology that seemed to contribute to their learning, but most have no "boundary object" to carry with them as they engage in future experiences, and we suspect they are less likely to build upon and extend their learning across future program experiences without such products. Even Miranda and Samantha may not build upon these experiences in goal-directed ways, without encouragement and an overall structure for doing so.[8]

CONCLUSION

Like many teacher educators, we face dramatically increased expectations for the quality of preparation of new teachers, which include preparing teacher candidates to use information technologies as professional and pedagogical tools. Like other teacher educators, we are exploring portfolio processes as means both to increase the coherence and power of our program and to conduct individual and program assessment. In addition, like others, we are exploring whether those portfolio processes can be served by information technology. Our faculty decided to infuse work with information technology into existing courses, and is exploring how we might construct some portfolio processes across the program as a whole. However, we are adopting an incremental approach that allows us to look closely at the educative value of such efforts.

We began these pilot efforts aiming to engage teacher candidates in authentic, goal-oriented portfolio processes that motivate and support professional learning, and that employ information technology as tools. We wanted to embed portfolio processes in the central tasks and activities of our courses and thereby implement them from the ground up instead of from the outside in. We wanted to make it more likely that the affordances of information technology would contribute to professional learning, and thus more likely that the technology used would be well learned and useful in the future. We wondered whether the portfolio processes and attendant technology would, in some unintended fashion, hinder rather than advance our efforts. We could argue that Erica's, Miranda's, and Samantha's cases were success stories only because they either entered with a fairly high level of technology proficiency or were taking a computing course simultaneously, and all had an intrinsic interest in learning more. We could argue further that these capacities and dispositions enabled them to take more risks and better use technology in pursuit of their own goals than others seemed to be able to do. On this reasoning, we would have to find ways to persuade future teacher candidates of the virtues of the course projects and the realistic power of some information technology, and to raise the technical support for meeting the technology's demands. We would approach that from the position that learning to construct portfolios is a developmental process (Winsor et al., 1999). If teacher candidates are to engage in authentic and goal-directed portfolio processes, we need to design our curriculum, assignments and assessment in ways that scaffold their learning and participation over time.

Alternatively, we could let Kathy's case remind us that most of the teacher candidates entered the courses willing to learn about technology and its uses, and that they coped with using technology fairly well. We found that the information technology we used, as we used it, generally did not overwhelm teacher candidates or obscure the substantive work of assignments. With modest course time devoted to supporting skill development, teacher candidates perceived that their skills increased and that they could use the selected technology as a learning tool. This leads us to think there may be merit in creating more uniformly ambitious technology-supported course requirements that engage teacher candidates in portfolio process across our program as whole.

We hope that our faculty's approach to portfolios remains incremental for a time yet. Crafting course assignments and engaging their technological support from the ground up has enabled us to maintain our concentration on the *professional learning processes* that technology-supported portfolio construction should serve. Perhaps we can design portfolio processes that

96 C.L. ROSAEN and T. BIRD

allow each course's tasks and content to take center stage during different parts of the program, while still focusing our teacher candidates' attention on coherent pursuit of longer-term aims across separate courses. As we continue to work with this conceptual framework, we plan to invite other program faculty to think and work with us to incorporate complementary experiences across the junior, senior and internship years.

NOTES

1. Before entering Michigan State University's Teacher Preparation Program, students take two teacher education courses as introductions to educational psychology, and school and society. Upon formal acceptance into the program in their junior year, they enroll in TE 301, Learners and Learning, which in the authors' teacher preparation team focuses on classroom management and lesson planning. During their senior year, they take block methods courses in literacy and math, and science and social studies. They spend about 4 hours per week observing, tutoring, teaching lessons, and assessing in the same classroom across the year. During their post-baccalaureate internship year novices work with collaborating teachers in classrooms 4–5 days per week. Simultaneously, they take two masters-level courses per semester that continue to support them in planning and teaching in the four subject matters emphasized in earlier courses. These courses also address inquiry and professional roles.

2. TeachersFile, a multimedia database built with Filemaker Pro 5.0 and piloted in the fall of 2000, provides teacher candidates a paperless workspace to support their work in the teacher preparation program.

3. Follow-up interviews with selected TE 401 teacher candidates were conducted in spring semester to gain more extensive understanding of these areas, but results are not included in this report.

4. The rating rubric rewarded clarity and orientation toward students in goals, validity and imagery in the expression of individual options for thought and action gleaned from the course, thoroughness balanced with compactness in capturing the set of options available, intelligent use of keywords to make options readily retrievable, reasonableness of declared relationships between options and goals, and overall impression of the File as an aid.

5. Wenger (1998) drew upon the work of sociologist of science Leigh Star to define boundary object as, "...artifacts, documents, terms, concepts, and other forms of reification around which communities of practice can organize their interconnections" (pp. 105–106).

6. The Survey of Computer Technology Uses was constructed using a framework developed by Bertram C. Bruce and James A. Levin (see: http://www.lis.uiuc.edu/%7Echip/pubs/taxonomy/index.html) where questions were organized around three categories: media for inquiry; media for communication; and media for expression.

7. These are questions we pursued in our follow-up interviews, but they are not included in this report.

8. One encouraging sign is that Miranda elected to continue with a second "honors option" and work further with the creation of electronic portfolios with first graders, and this will become part of her web page. She also has plans to use the portfolio template during her internship year.

REFERENCES

Anderson, L.M., & Bird, T. (1995). How three prospective teachers construed three cases of teaching. *Teaching and Teacher Education, 11*(5), 479–500.

Bird, T. (1990). The schoolteacher's portfolio: An essay on possibilities. In J. Millman & L. Darling-Hammond (Eds.), *Handbook of teacher evaluation: Elementary and secondary personnel* (2nd ed., pp. 241–256). Beverly Hills, CA: Sage Publications.

Bird, T., & Rosaen, C. (2001, April). *Teacher candidates learn to use information technology in portfolio work.* Paper presented at the annual meeting of the American Educational Research Association. Seattle, WA.

Bogdan, R.C., & Biklen, S.F. (1982). *Qualitative research for education: An introduction to theory and methods.* Boston: Allyn & Bacon.

Calderhead, J. (1991). The nature and growth of knowledge in student teaching. *Teaching and Teacher Education, 7*(5/6), 531–535.

Cambridge, B.L. (Ed.). (2001). *Electronic portfolios: Emerging practices in student, faculty, and institutional learning.* Washington, DC: American Association of Higher Education.

Dewey, J. (1938). *Experience and education.* New York: Macmillan.

Elliott, J. (1991). *Action research for educational change.* Philadelphia: Open University Press.

Erickson, F. (1986). Qualitative methods in research on teaching. In M.C. Whitrock (Ed.), *Handbook of research on teaching* (3rd ed., pp. 119–161). New York: Macmillan.

Georgi, D., & Crowe, J. (1998). Digital portfolios: A confluence of portfolio assessment and technology. *Teacher Education Quarterly, 25* (1), 73–84.

Gillingham, M.G., & Topper, A. (1999). Technology in teacher preparation: Preparing teachers for the future. *Journal of Technology and Teacher Education, 7* (4), 303–321.

International Society for Technology in Education. (1999). *National educational technology standards for students: Connecting curriculum and technology.* Eugene, OR: ISTE.

Interstate New Teacher Assessment and Support Consortium (INTASC). (1992). *Model standards for beginning teacher licensing: A resource for state dialogue.* Washington, DC: INTASC.

Johnson, J. (1999). Professional teaching portfolio: A catalyst for rethinking teacher education. *Action in Teacher Education, 21*(1), 37–49.

Keiffer, R.D., Hale, M.E., & Templeton, A. (1998). Electronic literacy portfolios: Technology transformations in a first-grade classroom. In D. Reinking, M.C. McKenna, & L.D. Labbo (Eds.), *Handbook of literacy and technology: Transforma-*

tion in a post-typographic world (pp. 145–163). Mahwah, NJ: Lawrence Erlbaum Associates.

Laffey, J., & Musser, D. (1998). Attitudes of preservice teachers about using technology and teaching. *Journal of Technology and Teacher Education, 6,* 223–241.

Lortie, D. (1975). *Schoolteacher: A sociological study.* Chicago: University of Chicago Press.

McKinney, M. (1998). Preservice teachers' electronic portfolios: Integrating technology, self-assessment, and reflection. *Teacher Education Quarterly, 25*(1), 85–103.

McLaughlin, M., & Vogt, M. (1996). *Portfolios in teacher education.* Newark, DE: International Reading Association.

McLaughlin, M., Vogt, M., Anderson, J.A., Du Mez, J., Peter, M., & Hunter, A. (1998). *Portfolio models: Reflections across the teaching profession.* Norwood, MA: Christopher-Gordon Publishers.

National Commission on Teaching and America's Future. (1996). *What matters most: Teaching for America's future.* New York: NCTA.

National Council for Accreditation of Teacher Education (NCATE). (1997). *Technology and the new professional teacher: Preparing for the 21st century classroom.* Washington, DC: NCATE.

Oja, S., & Smulyan, L. (1989). *Collaborative action research: A developmental approach.* New York: The Falmer Press.

Pintrich, P.R., Marx, R.W., & Boyle, R.A. (1993). Beyond cold conceptual change: The role of motivational beliefs and classroom contextual factors in the process of conceptual change. *Review of Educational Research, 63* (2), 167–199.

Reeves, T.C. (1996). Technology in teacher education: From electronic tutor to cognitive tool. *Action in Teacher Education, 17,* 74–78.

Rosaen, C. (Ed). (2001). *Guide to the elementary internship, 2001–02.* Teacher Preparation Team Two, Michigan State University, East Lansing, MI.

Wenger, E. (1998). *Communities of practice: Learning, meaning, and identity.* Cambridge: Cambridge University Press.

Wideen, M., Mayer-Smith, J., & Moon, B. (1998). A critical analysis of the research on learning to teach: Making the case for an ecological perspective on inquiry. *Review of Educational Research, 68*(2), 130–178.

Wigle, S.E., & White, G.T. (1998). Conceptual frameworks, portfolio assessment and faculty mentoring: Bridges to standards-based teacher education programs. *Action in Teacher Education, 20*(3), 39–49.

Wilcox, B., & Tomei, L. (1999). *Professional portfolios for teachers: A guide for learners, experts, and scholars.* Norwood, MA: Christopher-Gordon Publishers.

Willis, J., & Mehlinger, H. (1996). Information technology and teacher education. In J. Sikula, T.H. Butter, & E. Guyton (Eds.), *Handbook on research in teacher education* (pp. 978–1029). New York: Simon and Schuster Macmillan.

Winsor, P., Butt, R., & Reeves, H. (1999). Portraying professional development in preservice teacher education: Can portfolios do the job? *Teachers and Teaching: Theory and Practice, 5*(1), 9–19.

Wolf, K., & Dietz, M. (1998). Teaching portfolios: Purposes and possibilities. *Teacher Education Quarterly, 25*(1), 9–22.

CHAPTER 7

NOT "WHAT" BUT "HOW"

Becoming Design-wise
About Educational Technology

Punyashloke Mishra and Matthew J. Koehler

INTRODUCTION

Educational technology is here to stay. Although arguments about the promises and perils of educational technology abound, no one seriously questions that computers and other new information technologies will play an important role in the lives and learning of teachers and students. New technologies are already a significant presence in classrooms and schools. The numbers tell the story in no uncertain terms. Becker (1999) reported that between 1992 and 1998 the numbers of computers in U.S. schools grew more than 150%—from 3.5 million to 8.6 million. The ratio of students to computers dropped from 14 students for every computer in 1992, to six students per computer in 1998. More than 90% of schools have access to the Internet, with more than a third having direct access in classrooms.

How these computers are used is another matter. Despite the increased availability of computers and access to network resources, instructional use of new technology is quite limited. Less than half of the teachers with class-

What Should Teachers Know About Technology?: Perspectives and Practices, pages 99–121
Copyright © 2003 by Information Age Publishing
All rights of reproduction in any form reserved.

room Internet access in Becker's (1999) survey had students use the Web as a research tool on at least three occasions during the academic year. Only 7% of these teachers allowed students to use the computers to send e-mail as an instructional tool, and "even fewer involved the students in cross-classroom collaborative projects or in Web publishing" (p. 4).

Cuban (1999) found that fewer than two out of ten teachers are serious users of technology in the classroom. However, this is not because teachers are luddites or lack training. The "technology puzzle" according to Cuban is that, "of those same 10 American teachers, about seven have computers at home and use them to prepare lessons, communicate with colleagues and friends, search the Internet, and conduct personal business. In short, most teachers use computers at home more than at school."

What stands between reality and the vision of teachers creatively using technology in the classrooms of the future? The answer to this problem may seem straightforward—teachers need to know more about technology and how to use it in their classrooms. We argue that the problem is more complex—it is not simply a matter of *what* teachers need to know, but *how* they are supposed to learn it.

THE WHAT

Much has been written about what teachers need to know about technology to be effective teachers in the information age. Journal articles (Thomas, 1994; Widmer & Amburgey, 1994), state technology plans, and national standards have compiled a long list of the competencies that teachers will need to know in order to become skillful in technology-rich classrooms. These sources aptly list a wide range of competencies for teachers to master, including concrete skills (e.g., keyboarding, connecting a computer to the network); software application (e.g., word processing, spreadsheets); key technology concepts (e.g., networking, distributed computing); and transformative uses of technology in the classroom (e.g., learner-centered inquiry, using real-time data).

The voices are many, and include national, state, and local organizations, licensing agencies, professional organizations, and teacher preparation programs (Handler & Strudler, 1997; Hirumi & Grau, 1996; National Council for Accreditation of Teacher Education, 1997; Petrakis, 1997; U.S. Congress Office of Technology Assessment, 1995; Wiebe & Taylor, 1997). Kent and McNergney (1999) report that the teacher certification process in more than 32 states in the United States includes an explicit technology requirement. Most states have also developed technology plans that offer detailed idealized and prescriptive views of how technology should be used in classrooms (Zhao & Conway, 2001).

Technology standards, like other educational standards, tend to shape the curriculum and requirements of teacher preparation programs. Early versions of such technology standards for teachers have been criticized for being laundry lists of functional skills and knowledge that often ignored the situational and contextual realities of using technology for learning and teaching (Bruce, 1999). Such standards often interpret technology proficiency as the acquisition of technical skills—the ability to use current versions of hardware and software. Lankshear (1997) described this emphasis as a form of applied technocratic rationality, a view that technology is self-contained, has an independent integrity, and that to unlock its potential and power requires merely learning certain basic skills. Underlying these lists was the implicit assumption that teachers who can demonstrate proficiency with software and hardware will be able to incorporate technology successfully into their teaching.

Some recent standards initiatives of note have moved away from this list of technology proficiencies view. The International Society for Technology (ISTE) and the National Council for Accreditation of Teacher Education (NCATE) are good examples of moving beyond advocating basic skills. The ISTE standards do contain a list of foundational skills for all teachers. However, these standards also enumerate a series of higher order goals that are essential for effective pedagogy with technology. In doing so, ISTE has provided glimpses of what can and should be achieved with these basic skills. These current standards are powerful influences on teacher education curriculum in the United States primarily because NCATE is the only body officially sanctioned by the U.S. Department of Education to accredit schools of education. As Thomas, Taylor, and Knezek (1993) reported, the combined power of the ISTE standards and NCATE recognition had a significant impact both on developing programs and on promoting change in the educational structure within three years of their first being proposed. The ISTE standards have also become the basis for receiving funding and continued support of a variety of programs. For instance, the U.S. Department of Education's Preparing Tomorrow's Teachers to Use Technology (PT3) program, now in its third year, has allocated millions of dollars to enhance teachers' use of technology. Proposals for these funds are evaluated in part for their drawing on licensing, certification, and accreditation standards developed by state agencies and national associations, with ISTE and NCATE being mentioned by name. The ISTE/NCATE standards have been recognized as de-facto standards in other countries as well (Thomas et al., 1993).

The newer standards (such as the ISTE/NCATE standards) have gone beyond advocating basic skills by emphasizing the pedagogical role that technology can play and the nature of teacher knowledge that is required to fully utilize technology for teaching and learning. That said, we believe that even these improved standards do not provide a complete answer to the problem at hand, and meet *just part* of the challenge of helping teachers become smarter and better users of technology.

THE HOW

HOW are teachers supposed to learn WHAT the standards say they need to know? Teachers have often been left to go it alone—Kent and McNergney (1999) reported that a mere 15% of U.S. teachers had 9 hours or more of technology training, despite an increased emphasis on teacher training and teacher professional development. Clearly, time, money and opportunities are part of the equation, but so are values, goals and methods.

Teacher education approaches must find ways to give teachers a wide range of skills that lead to technological know-how that can impact classroom teaching. Moreover, approaches must address how to help teachers develop a deeper understanding of the concepts and skills that are not limited to specific instances of technology. For example, training teachers to use narrow software packages not only makes their knowledge too specific to be applied broadly, but it also becomes quickly outdated. Technology is changing so fast, that any method that attempts to keep teachers up to date on the latest software, hardware, and terminology is doomed to create knowledge that is out of date every couple of years.

We argue that traditional methods of technology training for teachers— mainly workshops and courses—are ill-suited to produce the "deep understanding" that can insulate teachers from the changes brought on by rapidly changing technology. Inevitably, these approaches rely on a process whereby teachers become *consumers* of knowledge about technological tools, with the hope that chances to learn about today's hardware and software packages will allow teachers to use them in their classrooms. In this view, the role of technology is to create more tools for teachers and students to use, and the role of teacher preparation is to train teachers in the proper use of these tools.

There is more to teacher preparation than training teachers how to use tools—it requires appreciation of the complex set of interrelationships between artifacts, users, tools and practices. Teachers must reconsider their way of thinking about technology and their relationship to it. Teachers need ways to think about their relationship toward technology as being complex, dynamic and continuously evolving, through which they develop sophisticated and nuanced understandings of the capabilities of technology as well as its constraints.

We believe that effective technology users often find innovative and conceptually sophisticated (though not necessarily technologically sophisticated) solutions to authentic pedagogical problems through the creative reinterpretation and re-purposing of existing technologies. Doing so requires a willingness and ability to critically examine new tools in terms of their implications for standards-based teaching and learning in the classroom. Our concept of what teachers need to know also includes a belief that teachers' professional development is a career-long commitment and that developing a plan for continued development is essential to maintaining proficiency.

We propose an approach which we call *learning technology by design*. In this approach, teachers work collaboratively in small groups to develop technological solutions to pedagogical problems. Thus, they become producers (rather than users) of technology and are allowed to learn in ways that tie their knowledge of technology to its educational uses (e.g., authentic problem solving). Teachers focus on an educational issue or problem and seek to find ways to use technology to address it. In the traditional workshop or class approach, teachers are trained in the use of the newest tools that they might be able to use in their classroom. In the learning by design approach, in the context of solving a problem, teachers become the designers of the tools. Because their explorations of technology are tied to their attempts to solve educational problems, teachers learn "how to learn" technology and "how to think" about technology. Hence, teachers go beyond thinking of themselves as passive users of technological tools and begin thinking of themselves as active designers of technology.

The structure of the rest of the chapter is as follows. We begin by offering our conceptualization of the design process and how it should be taught. Three case studies are provided as examples of how we have used the learning by design approach in our classes of practicing teachers. We conclude with a description of how these three case studies are similar and different from each other as well as what lessons we can learn from them.

LEARNING TECHNOLOGY BY DESIGN

Technology presumes there is just one right way to do things and there never is. And when you presume there is just one right way to do things, of *course* the instructions begin and end exclusively with [one predetermined product]. . . . But if you have to choose among an infinite number of ways to put it together then the relation of the machine to you, and the relation of the machine and you to the rest of the world, has to be considered, because the selection from among many choices, the *art* of the work is just as dependent upon your own mind and spirit as it is upon the material of the machine. (Pirsig, 1974, p. 160)

Why Design?

A design activity is a project-based activity in which learners design authentic complex interactive artifacts that will be used either by the designers themselves or by some one else. The emphasis is on creating authentic artifacts—that is, artifacts that will actually be used by people (Harel, 1991). Design-based projects have involved the development of presentations, instructional software, simulations, publications, journals, and games (Carver, Lehrer, Connell, & Erickson, 1992; Kafai, 1995; Kafai & Resnick, 1996; Lehrer, 1991). With such projects, students learn both about design—through the process of developing complex artifacts—and a variety of academic disciplines, such as programming, social studies, language arts, and others.

Research and theory suggest that design-based activities provide a rich context for learning. Within the context of social constructivism (Cole, 1997; Vygotsky, 1978) or constructionism (Harel & Papert, 1991), design projects lend themselves to sustained inquiry and revision of ideas. Other scholars have emphasized the value of complex, self-directed, personally motivated and meaningful design projects for students (Blumenfeld, Soloway, Marx, Krajcik, Guzdial, & Palincsar, 1991; Harel & Papert, 1990; Kafai, 1995). Such design-based informal learning environments offer a sharp contrast to regular classroom instruction, the effectiveness of which has been questioned by many scholars (Harel & Papert, 1991; Lave & Wenger, 1991 Papert, 1993; Pea, 1993). As one might imagine, adapting such open-ended problem solving situations into the structure and organization of the conventional classroom is often difficult.

Design, broadly speaking, can be seen as "structure adapted to a purpose" (Perkins, 1986, p. 2). Perkins' definition captures elegantly an essential quality of design: It is a process of constructing artifacts that exhibit "goodness of fit" (p. 2). The notion of fit is particularly appealing to us, because evaluating fit requires a more nuanced view of the conceptual domain—a view that is sensitive to complex set of interrelationships between artifacts, users, tools and practice. Design can be seen both in material artifacts, such as a hammer or a piece of software, as well as in nonmaterial artifacts, such as a poem, a theory or a scientific experiment.

Unfortunately, design has often been viewed as the formulaic application of a series of predetermined steps that must be accomplished in order to achieve a particular, pre-specified goal. At the heart of this assumption is what Donald Schön (1983) calls the "model of technical rationality" (p. 21). This model assumes that developing technology consists of "instrumental problem solving made rigorous by the application of scientific theory and technique" (p. 21). Dasgupta (1996) makes a similar point about the subservient relationship of technology to pure science when he says that too often technology is seen to be "merely the application of the relevant basic sciences to the making of artifacts" (p. 4).

More recently, it has been argued that design is more than the rote application of scientific knowledge to a given real world problem (Dasgupta, 1996; Gelernter, 1999; Mishra, Zhao, & Tan, 1999; Schön, 1983; Winograd, Bennett, De Young, & Hartfield, 1996). As Mishra et al. (1999) say:

> Design is a creative activity that cannot be fully reduced to standard steps, and should not be thought of as mere problem solving. A designer lacks the comforting restraints of a well-organized discipline because designing is inherently a messy endeavor. It includes, but goes beyond, the ability to be creative in solving problems. A host of techniques and skills come into play during design. Many of the techniques and skills are explicit and publicly available, while others may be tacit and unspoken. According to Smith and Tabor (1996), design is as much an art as it is a science—spontaneous, unpredictable, and hard to define. (p. 221)

Design requires a balancing act between a wide range of factors that often work against each other (features vs. cost, ease of use vs. advanced features, time to market vs. product quality, etc.). It requires the application of a wide array of knowledge, including algorithms, understanding of users, rules of thumb, scientific "facts," and multidisciplinary connections. This inherent "messiness" of design is further complicated when we consider the design of an abstract artifact, such as an after-school program (Vyas & Mishra, 2002) or an on-line course (Koehler, Mishra, Hershey, & Peruski, In press; Mishra, Koehler, Hershey, & Peruski, 2001).

Vygotsky (1978) and Dewey (1934) emphasize the role of dialogue or interplay in learning—as the individual acts on the environment, the environment also acts upon the individual. Design activities bring this interplay directly into focus. It is fundamentally about ideas and transforming oneself and the world through the process of working with those ideas. That is, the environment constrains and thereby acts upon the artifact (and therefore the designers), and the introduction of new artifacts changes the environment. This is especially true of technological artifacts, which exist in a transactional relationship with the world, that is, the artifacts are designed according to the constraints of the environment and, in turn, once these artifacts enter the "real world" they change the very environment they were designed for. E-mail, is a good example of this. E-mail's features, conceptual metaphors, and core operations are adopted from the environment of traditional ("snail") mail. Likewise, e-mail has changed the nature of text-based communication in the information age. Hence, design is essentially a dialogue between ideas and world, theory and its application, a concept and its realization, tools and goals. We see this dialogue as being at the heart of true inquiry, involving as it does the construction of meaning and the evolution of understanding through a dialogic, transactional process.

Teaching Design

Despite our optimism around learning by design, we should also acknowledge that teaching design requires a shift in understanding. In fact, Schön (1987) lists a range of reasons arguing that design cannot be taught in conventional ways:

- Designing is a holistic skill. It must be grasped as a whole, by experiencing it in action. It cannot be broken down into parts which can be understood in isolation from each other.
- Design depends a great deal on recognition of design qualities. This recognition is not something that can be described. It must be learned by doing.
- Designing is a creative process in which a designer comes to see and do things in new ways. Therefore, no prior description of it can take the place of learning by doing.
- Descriptions of designing are likely to be perceived initially as confusing, vague, ambiguous, or incomplete. The clarification of these ambiguities depends on a dialogue in which understandings and misunderstandings are revealed through action.
- The gap between a description of design and the knowing-in-action that corresponds to it must be filled by reflection-in-action.

To the following we add that not all design (or project-based) activities have equal educational value. Merely giving students "something to construct" may keep them busy but it is unclear as to what pedagogical value exists in doing so.

The sum of these arguments points toward learning about design by *doing* design, and relying less on overt lecturing and traditional teaching. Thus, our courses rely more on implicit learning through an active engagement in the class activities. We have designed a number of activities that teachers do (both in and out of class) that address the subtleties of the design process while developing technological fluency in teachers. We present three cases of our use of the learning by design approach to teaching master's-level educational technology courses. Following the cases, we conclude with an overview of what teachers learn in our approach.

These examples were drawn over three different courses during a two-year span. Although each class had different course goals, there were a number of similarities across the examples. Most of the participants in these courses were working teachers, often with years of experience in the classroom. Early in the courses, we divided participants into working groups that were responsible for defining, designing, and refining a solution to a problem throughout the course of the semester. These courses had the usual assigned readings, discussion, and writings, but all of these are aimed at supporting the main activity of the class—the design and evaluation of the artifacts created by the design teams.

Direct instruction or training about a particular software or technology was rare, and was only offered when requested by the participants. Though we did have a limited number of lectures, they were limited to short periods (20 to 30 minutes). These mini-lectures occurred for two reasons. First, a piece of software or hardware would be demonstrated if the whole class would need to do something repeatedly in the class (e.g., uploading their web pages to a server or operating a digital camera). Second, there were short discussions focused on big and powerful ideas about computing technology, such as the idea of a client-server relationship, internet protocols, file formats and hierarchical file structures, and digitization. The emphasis here was on understanding basic concepts and on connecting these concepts to the projects teachers were working on. In addition, these lectures often came toward the middle of the semester after teachers felt the need for a better understanding of these topics.

Instead of instructor-driven teaching about technology, the participants were free to choose (and often did so) any software or technology that they felt was important to solving their unique set of problems. This de-emphasis on particular computer programs or platforms meant that teachers often used a wide range of technologies and this in turn significantly changed the role of the instructor, since it was impossible for the instructor to be knowledgeable about all of the technologies being used by the different groups. The instructor was no longer a lecturer, and instead became a facilitator and a resource (albeit limited by his or her knowledge).

We offer below three instantiations of these ideas. The cases present some diversity around the theme of learning technology by design. Although these courses build on a similar set of principles and ideas, they do differ from each other in some respects. These differences, we believe, are not differences in philosophy about the design approach. Rather, they are the result of three main factors: (a) differences within faculty members in charge of the courses, (b) differences in course content and instructional goals, and finally (c) differences in institutional constraints, such as meeting-times, number of meetings in a week, and availability of electronic discussion groups. The three case studies allow us to see the same ideas play out across multiple contexts and identify commonalities and exceptions.

Case I: Faculty Development and On-line Learning

In the fall of 2001, Michigan State University began offering a master's degree program available entirely on-line. In order to prepare university faculty to meet the demands of teaching and learning in an on-line environment, institutions of higher education, such as Michigan State University, must find ways to develop the expertise needed to teach in the on-line world, while meeting several very real constraints (e.g., limited faculty time, limited college budgets, or fear of technology). The standard approach to confronting these problems is to enlist the help of technical experts (e.g., web programmers) for the technical aspects of on-line course development, and leave the pedagogy to the experts in their chosen fields. Unfortunately, in this approach, the web programmers may end up making decisions that have unintended pedagogical consequences. Pedagogical experts, unfamiliar with the technology, may not recognize the subtleties of how technical decisions can affect pedagogy. We attempted to solve this problem of developing on-line courses *and* of faculty professional development using the learning by design approach. Instead of handing the web programmers a set of materials that worked in the face-to-face classroom, we advocate that the expert teachers take a hand in the design of the technology to support the learning. We relied on the process of design to develop the necessary skills and relationships for understanding the nuances of integrating technology and pedagogy and the complexities of applying the knowledge thus gained to the complex domain of real world practice.

This faculty professional development was achieved through a regular master's level course in educational technology co-taught by the authors. We extended membership in this course to include six tenured faculty members, who enrolled as "students" in the design course. Teams consisting of one faculty member and three or four master's students worked on designing an on-line course that would be taught by the faculty member in the following year. The major activities of the course consisted of readings, explorations with technology, prototyping of the on-line course, on-line and in-class discussions, and peer review and feedback. A typical class period had a whole-group component that was used to discuss readings and issues that applied to all groups, and a small-group component in which the design teams worked on their projects.

In many ways, this design course was a typical graduate class experience for the teachers—they read articles, discussed ideas, and were responsible for meeting course deadlines. However, there were some important differences. Like faculty members, teachers were exposed to several technologies, assessed their usefulness, and potentially used them in the design of the on-line class. In more traditional technology courses, all teachers explicitly learn the same target technologies as part of the course (e.g., web design, digital video). In contrast, the design approach made learning about technology implicit—teachers learned about technologies, as they needed to, in order to fulfill some desired feature of the course they were designing. However, despite this implicit approach, teachers were exposed to a range of different technologies and managed to focus their attention on particular technologies that were most appropriate for the task at hand. The choices of technologies used by the groups varied, depending on the design of their on-line course. One group, for instance, focused a great deal on understanding how a faculty member could provide audio feedback to his students. Another group investigated the use of PowerPoint presentations via the Web to offer overviews of the lessons to be covered. Groups also explored a range of pedagogical issues such as developing techniques for developing a learning community on-line as well as strategies for problem-based learning. All of the groups learned about the nature of effective web design as part of putting their course on-line for review and feedback. Apart from issues of technology, the faculty-student groups also learned about other issues of on-line course design such as copyright and privacy. This knowledge was shared with the larger class through whole groups discussions as well as through on-line critiques of work done by other groups.

The task of designing an on-line course was a unique opportunity for most teachers. None of the students had previously had the opportunity to design a graduate course. Seeing and participating in the process of developing a graduate level course from scratch provided the students with a opportunity to apply their knowledge of educational theory to a real-world context, and thus further their own development as future lecturers, instructors, and professors. As one student-participant said, "This class has been one that I will never forget. From how much work building, maintaining, and revising an on-line course is to learning how to work in a group again, this experience has been one that has reshaped many things that I have held to or thought about teaching."

In addition, the chance to work with tenured faculty provided novel experiences for most of the students. Too often, graduate students' experiences with their professors seem opaque—they only get to see final products of their thought processes (e.g., research papers, courses they take). By working with expert educators, they were able to interact with ideas in ways that they are seldom allowed. They worked over a whole semester with these ideas, and were able to influence the experts' ideas and apply them to a real problem. Most student participants reported that this course was one of the best that they had ever had in their graduate program. Working on an authentic design problem, within a group led by a faculty member made the experience unique—one very different from most courses the students had been in before.

Case II: Making Movies in Switzerland

As the capstone sequence toward a master's in educational technology, the second author and Dr. David Wong taught a nine-credit, educational technology sequence to 28 teachers. Their goals were to give teachers additional insight into the fields of educational psychology and educational technology, and how the two fields interact in expert practice. Again, much of the course was traditional—the participants had assigned readings, discussion groups about readings, some lecturing about educational issues, and action research projects to do. However, part of the course goals was to learn some concrete, advanced technology skills. In this course, the teachers were to learn the ins and outs of digital video. The instructors decided to accomplish this goal with the learning by design approach (Wong, Mishra, Koehler, & Sibenthal, 2003).

Teachers had to make two movies, called *iVideos* (idea-based videos) to communicate an idea of education importance to a wider audience. The iVideos had to inspire others with passion for the idea. The first video had to complete the sentence: "Teaching is _____." The second video was up to the groups (with the approval of the instructors). Topics included, the role of technology in the library sciences, communicating on-line, and appropriate uses of technology. Instead of learning the de-contextualized skill of creating and editing digital video, the teachers had to learn the technology within the context of communicating a broad educational idea.

Teachers were provided with digital cameras, tapes, tripods, software, and computers. They also received a one-hour demo of how to use a camera, capture video, edit it, and produce a digital movie. Most of their time was spent in groups discussing or debating their idea, storyboarding, filming, digitizing, editing, revising, and soliciting feedback. The instructors scheduled regular times for teachers to preview their works in progress to the whole class and receive feedback. Versions of their iVideos were posted to a web site so that feedback from other master's-level courses could also serve as an impetus to change and redesign. Once the movies were complete, they were shown to an audience of approximately 80 other people involved in the summer session, and were posted to the web site so that people outside the summer school could also participate in the viewing and feedback.

The design approach often results in classrooms that look and feel quite different from traditional university offerings. This was especially true in this case, and is worth mentioning in detail. The teachers were never all in one place, and spread to other rooms of the school, the hallway, outside, and any other place they could find room to talk, film, edit, storyboard, argue, screen, and preview video. These activities went well beyond class time, teachers worked late into the night in the lab, in their dorms, and through the weekends.

The instructors did hardly any lecturing about the "nuts and bolts" of digital video, instead they spent most of their time circulating among the teachers, acting as a coach, guide, and mentor. Occasionally some advanced technical assistance was given by the instructor, but for the most part the teachers learned "how to learn" without the help of the instructors. They began to rely more and more on their fellow teachers, and undertook responsibility for their own learning by playing with the software and hardware, seeking out on-line resources and tutorials, and sharing their knowledge outwards to the other teachers. We hope that the teachers in our program will transfer these meta-level ideas of "learning how to learn" to their future interactions with technology.

Given that there was no list of skills that teachers needed to learn, nor was their grade based on learning specific skills, the list of technologies that were learned was impressive. These included skills, such as operating digital cameras (still and video); using video and image editing software (such as iVideo and Photoshop); conducting internet searches as well as uploading and downloading files (through FTP or other means); and design web pages using software such as Dreamweaver or FrontPage. Apart from these specific skills, students also learned key concepts in information technology, such as internet protocols, file formats and structure, video compression technologies (CoDecs) and others.

More important that their individual technology skills was their learning about the subtleties and relationships between and among tools, actors, and contexts. Technology was learned in the context of expressing educational idea and metaphors. For example, seven different metaphors were used and discussed for the "Teaching is _____" assignment. Teachers learned a lot about how to focus a message down to just two minutes of video, how to let images and symbolism convey ideas in an effective manner, how to inspire audiences, working together in groups, giving and receiving feedback, and communicating with audiences.

Case III: Learning Technology through Design

This course, a master's seminar in educational technology offered by the first author, dealt with technical, pedagogical, and social issues around design and educational uses of web-based technologies. Most participants in this graduate class were practicing K–12 teachers who brought their rich professional knowledge of teaching and learning to this course. Participants in this class were expected not only to learn interactive web-based technology but also generate abstract knowledge (about designing educational technology) through working in groups on four different design projects. In the learning process, each member of group was engaged in activities that compelled them to seriously study technology, education, the interface between the two, and the social dynamics of working with others.

Like the other two cases, teachers in this class did plenty of readings and discussion (both in-class and on-line).

The tasks assigned to this group were different from the projects in the two courses described previously. Participants in the previous courses were involved in the task of developing movies or on-line courses from scratch. In contrast, participants in this course were involved in the redesign of existing web sites or web resources. This emphasis on redesign was to ensure that the participants would not spend a lot of time researching the topic, but instead would focus on the process of design. Sixteen teachers were divided into four groups. Each group did one of the following redesign tasks: (a) redesign of the virtual tour of the College of Education, (b) redesign of a web publishing course for middle school students, (c) redesign of a children's computer clubhouse web site to make it more accessible to children and parents, and finally (d) redesign of a database on educational psychology theory and practice (currently available at http://tip.psychology.org). Each of these projects had a different audience, ranging from middle school students to visitors to the college of education web site; from parents of students at a computer clubhouse to master's or doctoral students in educational psychology. Teachers in this class also participated in whole class discussion, project presentations and critiques, asynchronous on-line discussion, journals, and final group reflection on design process.

The fact that the teachers were engaged in authentic design activities around educational technology compelled them to seriously study the complex relationships between technology and education. The redesign projects forced the participants to think deeply evaluating the needs of the audience and to configure their design to meet these needs. Thus, by the end of the semester teachers had learned valuable and self-affirming lessons about managing and learning in situations that were often ambiguous, confusing and frustrating.

Though one of the goals of these courses was to have participants learn technologies, the instructors did not specify what software programs the teachers were to use. In addition, teachers were offered no explicit training on particular software programs. Though this approach generated some frustration at the beginning, throughout the course, teachers had learned a wide number of technologies to complete their projects. For instance, the virtual tour group learned QuickTime VR, the web-publishing group used JavaScript in their web pages, the database group focused on database driven web sites, and the clubhouse group utilized a variety of site building and image manipulation tools. They did this by studying manuals, talking to each other, talking to the instructor, and seeking out other locally available experts. The range of technological knowledge these projects brought to bear often outstripped the knowledge of the instructors. In fact, this would be one of the few classes where the instructors learned as much from the teachers as the teachers learned from the instructor! This would not have been possible if the instructors had a-priori determined the range of software packages that would be covered.

An important part of the class was the electronic discussion. This was maintained through either a bulletin board or through a web-archived listserv. Teachers were asked to write two or three journals through the semester. The timings of the journals were staggered in order to have regular postings to the group throughout the semester. Teachers were not constrained in any way about the topics they could raise though they were encouraged to connect the journals to issues currently being raised in the class. Teachers were also asked to supply constructive criticisms of the products being developed by the other groups. This helped develop a sense of community as well as allow for in-depth discussions on topics—something not necessarily possible in the regular class time.

WHAT WAS LEARNED

The three case studies presented here all used the learning by design approach to help teachers learn about educational technology. Though there were some important differences between these courses, they do capture the spirit of the learning by design approach. Across the three settings, we argue that the teachers learned quite a bit about technology, about design, and about learning.

Learning About Technology

In each of the three case studies, it is clear that teachers (and instructors) covered a wide range of technology skills and concepts. If all the skills learned were listed together, the list would be impressively long. Rather than focus on *what* hardware and software skills were learned, we wish to speak to *what* teachers learned about subtleties and complexities of technology in education. These are briefly summarized below.

Technologies have affordances and constraints.   One feature of learning by design is that, as designers, teachers must confront the affordances and constraints of technology (Gibson, 1986; Norman, 1993). The design tasks enforce some constraints, including the time to complete the project, the expected audience, and the tools available to complete the job. Most decisions that a design team makes have to consider these strengths and limitations of particular technologies—deciding whether to lay out an on-line course conceptually or chronologically, whether to use one teacher's idea or another's for imagery in an iVideo, or whether to use a particular graphical editor in designing the web sites.

Technologies are context sensitive.   In the design activities, technologies are investigated, evaluated, and applied in order to accomplish a goal. Hence, technologies were always learned within the context of the task. In some sense, the context was the same for all teachers—they were learning about technology within the larger context of a master's course (or courses). However, because of differences in the personnel, goals, resources available, and the faculty involved, the context could vary significantly. This is particularly important when we consider the malleable nature of the digital computer (Papert, 1980) that affords multiple uses depending on the context. For example, in case one (on-line course development) one group learned how to use PowerPoint to communicate their progress to other groups. A second group explored advanced features of PowerPoint to make on-line lectures come alive by synchronizing audio with bulleted topical summaries of key points. In short, in design activities such as these, providing context is never a problem because context provides the grounding for *all* learning.

Technologies are social actors.   In design approaches, technologies are never passive, and they are a part of the larger design context. As Brey (1997) says, "Artifacts can have effects because they can act, just like human beings. Consequently, they can also have unintended effects, just like an individual can perform actions that were neither intended nor anticipated by others." Schön (1996) talks about the idea of backchat where the design talks back to the designer. As Schön describes it, the designer needs to listen to the design and to determine his or her next moves based on this knowledge. It is while in the process of designing that designer learns about the kinds of moves that need to be made to solve the problem. In certain situations, this may lead to redefining the problem itself. For instance, as the educational psychology database group continued to work on their design, they realized that users would often want to print out the contents of the pages. This required them to rethink the design in a very fundamental manner and to offer the option of printer-friendly pages. Thus, the process of design becomes a conversation—a mutually constituted negotiation between the developing artifact and evolving conceptions of the designers.

Technologies are malleable.   Naïve users of technology often use technology in stereotypical ways. However, an immediate consequence of the idea that the computer is a protean machine is the fact that it is a malleable device. The overarching goal of design is to get the artifact to "do the job" within the constraints of time and resources available. This often pressures designers to creatively re-purpose the tools and resources in hand if they are to achieve their goals. There were many such examples of re-purposing visible during the design projects. Freely downloadable JavaScripts that were meant to display random quotes were redesigned to display random images instead. Since sharing large amounts of video data over the network was not feasible, the teachers making iVideos came up with the creative solution of "dumping" their partially edited materials back to tape and digitizing it again onto another computer. Hence, the camera and tape became re-purposed to serve as a mass storage device. To these teachers, a piece of technology is no longer viewed as a tool for doing just one thing; it has a range of potential uses (even some that have not been considered yet).

Technology means breakdowns.   In the technology-rich design environments we described, opportunities for teachers to learn about the breakdowns associated with technology were not hard to find. For example, every day the video design teams constantly faced breakdowns, minor bugs, and major flaws associated with Adobe Premiere. Teachers had to learn ways around these bugs to complete their projects and often shared tips with their fellow teachers (defragmenting the hard drive, configurations of memory and virtual memory, suggested sequences of actions to take in the software to avoid crashes, etc.). Teachers in the web site redesign course faced innumerable problems due to incompatible software programs where work done by one teacher with FrontPage (for example) would not be accessible by another teacher with Dreamweaver, and when a perfectly designed web page would "vanish" when uploaded.

These breakdowns were wonderful teachable moments allowing the instructors to talk about larger and bigger issues of file formats, hierarchical file structures, and client-server relationships. A previous abstract and abstruse discussion on file naming conventions becomes important when teachers are faced with the immediate problem of images not showing up on their web pages. Moreover, it was not that the instructors were immune to such breakdowns. These happened often and were another instance where a possible problem could be seen as instructionally valuable. These situations allowed the instructors to model appropriate responses—how to trouble shoot, how to work through a problem, when to ask for help and when to stop and fall back on another technology.

Learning About Design

Design is not something that can be taught by lectures and demonstrations. It is learned best through the active process of creating and doing. That said, design is hard to learn. It can be extremely motivating, enjoyable, and frustrating at the same time. The fact that there are no magic solutions, and even the solutions that emerge are compromises at best, is often a difficult message to swallow. By involving teachers in these design projects, we offered them an opportunity to explore and play within the relatively "consequence-free" zone of a classroom. In some sense, the classroom became a laboratory for teachers to experiment and try out different concepts, to experiment with technologies and ideas.

Design is for a purpose. An important lesson to learn is that design is always for a purpose. Thinking of this forces designers (as it did the participants in our courses) to take on a variety of perspectives on their design. Continual feedback (both formal and informal, from the instructors and from their fellow teachers) forced them to think of their work from the point of view of the users (be they students, or teachers or parents). This perspective taking is an extremely important part of design. For example, teachers in the web redesign groups tested their designs on groups of potential users and this feedback was invaluable in revealing assumptions and gaps that they were not aware of initially.

Design is iterative. Participants also developed a better understanding of the conversational and dialogic nature of design. An important part of design is that of redesign—of going back to the first principles and thinking about every decision that they made. Participants became sensitive to the consequences of their initial decisions since the consequences of these initial decisions could ripple through their work and sometime constrain them in ways they had not initially envisaged. For instance, the choice of a software program for web design, if not thought through carefully, could wreak havoc on the final design, as did happen to the group redesigning the clubhouse web site. Thus, design became a series of ongoing experiments—a process of intentional variation and selective retention of those experiments that worked and rejection of those that did not.

That is, design is best characterized as a cycle—it never really ends. There are temporary points of closure, often dictated by external constraints such as the time available. Most teachers in these design-oriented courses became sensitive to these issues as they became more involved in their projects, hoping to develop a perfect product. They realized that their projects could, in some sense, go on forever but that often the best that can be achieved is "satisficing"—doing the best they could with what they had in the time available (Simon, 1969). The deadline of the final presentation to a large group urged them to complete their projects. Though the design teams were often quite critical of their own work, it was always interesting for them to see how people outside the class viewed their work. It was rarely if ever seen as incomplete.

Design is eclectic. Design is a pragmatic exercise. It is a search for solutions that work. In attempting to achieve this, design is eclectic, in that it does not respect traditional disciplinary boundaries. This is because real-world problems are often not contained with such boundaries either and hence coming up with a solution requires thinking outside of these restrictions. For instance participants in the web redesign course had to think about the psychology of human computer interaction, the nature of the content they were presenting, as well as the constraints of the technology (i.e., software and hardware) and more. Any decision in one area (say the choice of a navigational structure for the site) would have consequences for all of these domains. A special JavaScript pull-down menu could possibly solve the problem of navigation and use of space on the screen but would restrict the kinds of browsers that could view the site.

Design is complex. Teachers became sensitive to the fact that every choice made by a designer has both intended and unintended consequences. Design thus is not so much a process of planning and executing, as it is a conversation. It is a conversation in which the conversing partner—the designed object itself—generates unexpected interruptions and contributions. The process of design can be fruitfully seen as an ongoing series of experiments in which the self and the object to be constructed are in continuous dialogue. The designer has to listen to the emerging design, even while shaping it. This dialogue often happens at multiple levels, between theory and practice, between constraints and tradeoffs, between the designer and the materials and between participants in the group.

Learning About Learning

The classrooms these teachers found themselves in looked a lot different than the classrooms they typically encounter. Instead of sitting in rows, facing the instructor, these classrooms have multiple foci of activity, as teaches worked in groups. When teachers talk about problems they are facing in their designs, fellow teachers are just as likely to have ideas for solutions as instructors are. We hope that this view of learning and teaching would be something that the participants in our classroom would carry with them even after they graduated. We list below some of the key aspects of the learning by design experience:

Learning is frustrating and challenging. Design projects involving technology can be extremely frustrating. There are many reasons for this. One reason was that teachers were concurrently learning the very technologies they were using to develop their final projects. This, when combined with the tendency of technology to break down, could make the process quite unsettling and frustrating.

Design is also difficult because solutions are not easy to develop: Every potential solution has competing solutions, and deciding between the possibilities is not easy. Being left, for the most part, on their own and responsible for their own learning, was often not something most of the participants had expected or had much experience with. Despite the fact that these were practicing teachers and master's students, many of them expected to be given direct lessons on what to do, which menu to pull down, and which buttons to click, to complete a particular task. Re-orienting their view about what teaching and learning looks like (even at the master's level) was not always easy.

Learning is fun.   Despite the fact that design was frustrating; it was also intensely motivating and fun. In the learning by design approach, the classrooms we described all generated a buzz that is hard to characterize—there is a certain energy and mood to the classroom that becomes part of the context. Learning becomes fun again. As one teacher noted, "I think, in most situations, people don't want to learn, or don't like learning because learning is boring and monotonous. However, in this class, learning is meaningful and also fun and enjoyable."

Learning is an active process.   Teachers often came into these courses expecting to learn to use technology. This meant that they often perceived themselves as consumers of knowledge. However, in these courses they were put in the role of generating knowledge not just consuming it. They had to come up with answers to questions and dilemmas that arose during the design process. Instructors are put in the role of coaches and guides, and less in the role of the keeper of answers. Initially, many teachers felt uncomfortable with this position—often wondering why the instructors would not simply tell them the answer. Over time, teachers begin to investigate potential technologies for themselves, use the Web to search for resources and ideas, and learn to ask questions to the entire group. In short, they begin to understand that learning is a community of practitioners (in which they are an equal part), and not a process of communicating knowledge from a few experts (the instructors) to the novices (the teachers).

After a while, many teachers picked up the new rhythm of the classroom, and began to see the power of their being in charge. Comments like the following were not uncommon: "This experience has been one that has reshaped many things that I have held to or thought about teaching."

Learning happens in a range of contexts, both inside and outside of classrooms.   One of the most interesting consequences of the learning by design projects was that learning was no longer restricted to the classroom. Teachers often met outside of the classroom in groups or brought their own individual investigations and experiments to share with the group. These courses changed from being just the completion of a set of requirements for receiving a master's degree to something to which students looked forward. This aspect of learning outside of class can be best seen in the journal postings (and responses) in the web site redesign course. Discussions on the listserv were wide-ranging and engaging, and delved deeply into issues such as the aesthetics of design, design and its relationship to teaching, and the impact of new technologies on schools. This allowed deeper and wider conversations than could have been possible through the regular class meetings.

CONCLUSIONS

We began this paper with the question of what do teachers need to know. We argued that though we are increasingly become sensitive to WHAT teachers need to know we need to get a better sense of HOW they are to learn it. Understanding that technology is more than the accumulation of skills, and that skillful teaching is more the science of applying the right tool for the job. We have offered above one possibility—the idea of "learning by design"—where teachers learn about educational technology by doing educational technology. Design, we argued, was necessarily a complex interplay between tools, artifacts, individuals and contexts. Design activities allow teachers to explore the ill-structured domain of educational technology and develop flexible ways of thinking about technology.

ACKNOWLEDGMENTS

Contributions of the two authors to this article were equal. We rotate authorship in our writing.

We would like to thank a number of people who in different ways have helped us conceptualize these ideas. In particular Punya would like to thank Yong Zhao for his willingness to experiment with the design teams idea more than three years ago. Matthew would like to thank David Wong for co-teaching in the Summer of 2001 in Leysin, Switzerland. We would both like to thank all the students in our classes. Their excitement and enthusiasm has been the single most important motivation for trying these ideas.

The work has been partially funded by a PT3 grant awarded to Michigan State University.

REFERENCES

Becker, H.J. (1999). Internet use by teachers: Conditions of professional use and teacher-directed student use. *Report of the teaching, learning, and computing: 1998 national survey.* Center for Research on Information Technology and Organizations, The University of California, Irvine and The University of Minnesota.

Blumenfeld, P., Soloway, E., Marx, R., Krajcik, J., Guzdial, M., & Palincsar, A. (1991) Motivating project-based learning: Sustaining the doing, supporting the learning. *Educational Psychologist, 26* (3&4), 369–398.

Brey, P. (1997). Philosophy of technology meets social constructivism. *Techné: Journal of the Society for Philosophy and Technology. 2*, 3–4, 56–79.

Bruce, B.C. (1999). Speaking the unspeakable about 21st century technologies. In G. Hawisher & C. Selfe (Eds.), *Passions, pedagogies, and 21st century technologies* (pp. 221–228). Logan: Utah State University Press.

Carver, S.M., Lehrer, R., Connell, T., & Erickson, J. (1992). Learning by hypermedia design: Issues of assessment and implementation. *Educational Psychologist, 27*(3), 385–404.

Cole, M. (1997). *Cultural psychology: A once and future discipline.* Cambridge, MA: The Belknap Press of Harvard University Press.

Cuban, L. (1999). The technology puzzle. *Education Week on the Web.* http://www.edweek.org/ew/1999/43cuban.h18

Dasgupta, S. (1996). *Technology and creativity.* New York: Oxford University Press.

Dewey, J. (1934). *Art as experience.* New York: Perigree.

Gelernter, D.H. (1999). *Machine beauty: Elegance at the heart of technology.* New York: Basic Books.

Gibson, J.J. (1986). *The ecological approach to visual perception.* Mahwah, NJ: Lawrence Erlbaum Associates.

Handler, M.G., & Strudler, N. (1997). The ISTE foundation standards: Issues of implementation. *Journal of Computing in Teacher Education, 13*(2), 16–23.

Harel, I. (1991). *Children designers: Interdisciplinary constructions for learning and knowing mathematics in a computer-rich school.* Norwood, NJ: Ablex.

Harel, I., & Papert, S. (1990). Software design as a learning environment. *Interactive Learning Environments, 1*(1), 1–32.

Harel, I., & Papert, S. (1991). *Constructionism.* Norwood, NJ: Ablex.

Hirumi, A., & Grau, I. (1996). A review of computer-related state standards, textbooks, and journal Articles: Implications for preservice teacher education and professional development. *Journal of Computing in Teacher Education, 12*(4), 6–17.

Kafai, Y.B. (1995). *Minds in play: Computer game design as a context for children's learning.* Hillsdale, NJ: Lawrence Erlbaum Associates.

Kafai, Y.B., & Resnick, M. (1996). *Constructionism in practice: Designing, thinking, and learning in a digital world.* Hillsdale, NJ: Lawrence Erlbaum Associates.

Kent, T.W., & McNergney, R.F. (1999). *Will technology really change education?: From blackboard to web.* Thousand Oaks, CA: Corwin Press.

Koehler, M.J., Mishra, P., Hershey, K., & Peruski, L. (in press). With a little help from your students: A new model for faculty development and online course design. *Journal of Technology and Teacher Education.*

Lankshear, C. (1997) *Changing literacies.* Buckingham & Philadelphia: Open University Press.

Lave, J., & Wenger, E. (1991). *Situated learning: Legitimate peripheral participation.* Cambridge: Cambridge University Press.

Lehrer, R. (1991). Authors of knowledge: Patterns of hypermedia design. In S. Lajoie & S. Derry (Eds.), *Computers as cognitive tools.* Hillsdale NJ: Lawrence Erlbaum Associates.

Mishra, P., Koehler, M.J., Hershey, K., & Peruski, L. (2001, November). *Learning through design: Faculty development and on-line course development.* Paper presented at the Seventh Sloan-C International Conference on Online Learning: Emerging Standards of Excellence in Asynchronous Learning Networks, Orlando, FL.

Mishra, P., Zhao, Y., & Tan, H.S. (1999). From concept to software: Unpacking the blackbox of design. *Journal of Research on Computing in Education, 32*(2), 220–238.

National Council for Accreditation of Teacher Education. (1997). *Technology and the new professional teacher: Preparing for the 21st century classroom.* Washington, DC: National Council for Accreditation of Teacher Education.

Norman, D. (1993). *Things that make us smart: Defending human attributes in the age of the machine.* New York: Addison-Wesley.

Papert, S. (1980). *Mindstorms: Children, computers, and powerful ideas.* New York: Basic Books.

Papert S. (1993). *Children's machine: Rethinking school in the age of the computer.* New York: Basic Books.

Pea, R.D. (1993). Practices of distributed intelligence and designs for education. In G. Salomon (Ed.), *Distributed cognitions* (pp. 47–87). New York: Cambridge University Press.

Perkins, D.N. (1986). *Knowledge as design.* Hillsdale, NJ: Lawrence Erlbaum Associates.

Petrakis, E. (1997). Using a portfolio to assess preservice teachers' technology competence. *Journal of Computing in Teacher Education, 13*(1), 12–13.

Pirsig, R.M. (1974). *Zen and the art of motorcycle maintenance.* New York: William Morrow & Company.

Schön, D. (1983). *The reflective practitioner.* London: Temple Smith.

Schön, D. (1987). *Educating the reflective practitioner.* San Francisco: Jossey-Bass.

Schön, D. (1996). Reflective conversation with materials. In T. Winograd, J. Bennett, L. De Young, B. Hartfield, (Eds.), *Bringing design to software* (pp. 171–184). New York: Addison-Wesley.

Simon, H.A. (1969). *The sciences of the artificial.* Cambridge, MA: The MIT Press.

Smith, G.C., & Tabor, P. (1996). The role of the artist-designer. In T. Winograd, J. Bennett, L. De Young, & B. Hartfield (Eds.), *Bringing design to software* (pp. 37–57). New York: Addison-Wesley.

Thomas, L. (1994). NCATE releases new unit accreditation guidelines: Standards for technology are included. *Journal of Computing in Teacher Education, 11*(3), 5–7. SP523918

Thomas, L.G., Taylor, H.G., & Knezek, D.G. (1993). National accreditation standards impact teacher preparation. *T.H.E. Journal,* 62–64.

U.S. Congress, Office of Technology Assessment (1995). *Teachers and technology: Making the connection* (OTA-EHR-616). Washington, DC: Office of Technology Assessment.

Vyas, S., & Mishra, P. (2002). Experiments with design in an after-school Asian literature club. In R. Garner, Y. Zhao, & M. Gillingham (Eds), *Hanging out: Community-based after-school programs for children.* Westport, CT: Bergin and Harvey.

Vygotsky, L.S. (1978). *Mind in society: The development of higher psychological processes.* Cambridge, MA: Harvard University Press.

Widmer, C.C., & Amburgey, V. (1994). Meeting technology guidelines for teacher preparation. *Journal of Computing in Teacher Education, 10*(2), 12–16. SP523575

Wiebe, J.H., & Taylor, H.G. (1997). What should teachers know about technology? A revised look at the ISTE foundations. *Journal of Computing in Teacher Education, 13*(3), 5–9.

Winograd T., Bennet J., De Young L., & Hartfield B. (1996). *Bringing design into software.* New York: Addison-Wesley.

Wong, D., Mishra, P., Koehler, M.J., & Siebenthal, S. (in press). Teacher as filmmaker: iVideos, technology education, and professional development. To appear in M. Girod & J. Steed (Eds.), *Technology in the college classroom.* Stillwater, OK: New Forums Press.

Zhao, Y., & Conway, P. (2001). What's in and what's Out?: An analysis of state technology plans. *Teachers   College   Record,*   http://www.tcrecord.org/Content.asp?ContentID=10717

CHAPTER 8

TEACHER KNOWLEDGE OF EDUCATIONAL TECHNOLOGY

A Case Study of Student/Mentor Teacher Pairs

Jon Margerum-Leys and Ronald W. Marx

INTRODUCTION

This study lies at the intersection of two critical currents in American education: A growing sense of the importance of the role of the teacher in the implementation of educational technology and the need to successfully prepare literally millions of new teachers in the coming decade. In this study, we argue that the role that teachers play is dependant in part on what they know and that in turn, what teachers know is impacted by their opportunities for learning.

The acquisition of knowledge regarding educational technology by student teachers and their mentors is the focus of this study. In general, computer-based technology is a major object of thought and action in the K–12 educational community (President's Committee of Advisors on Science and Technology Panel on Educational Technology, 1997). Technology use in

What Should Teachers Know About Technology?: Perspectives and Practices, pages 123–159
Copyright © 2003 by Information Age Publishing
123

education holds the promise of increased student performance (Wenglinsky, 1998), support of reform-oriented curriculum interventions (Means & Olson, 1995), and improved teacher professional communication (Gibson & King, 1997), among other educational benefits. Recent research has established a number of requirements that need to be addressed in order for the promise of technology to be realized (e.g., Krajcik, Soloway, Blumenfeld & Marx, 1998), prominent among these being adequate preparation for and support of teachers (Willis & Mehlinger, 1996). Despite the recognized importance of teacher preparation and development in technology use, little is known about how and what teachers learn through traditional professional development efforts (Wilson & Berne, 1999). In this study, we identify student teachers as a potential source of educational technology knowledge, exploring knowledge acquisition in ways that we believe can inform professional development as well as teacher preparation.

Intersecting the new opportunities offered by technology is a demand for a large number of new teachers; American schools will encounter a vast infusion of new teachers as tens of thousands of teachers retire and as new opportunities are created through forces such as larger student populations and legislation mandating smaller class sizes. If teacher education is equal to the challenge of meeting the demand for new teachers, these changes promise—among many other things—the opportunity to rapidly bring increased technological understanding to the classroom. Teachers entering the field of education have a responsibility to acquire the knowledge needed to be effective technology-using educators (CEO Forum, 1997), just as teacher educators have a responsibility to give these teachers the means to do so (Handler, 1993).

A central component of teacher preparation programs is the student teaching experience. Because learning to teach is in large measure a professional enterprise, it is essential that theoretical and practical knowledge develop in concert. Thus, student teaching is seen by many (e.g., Borko & Putnam, 1996; Carter, 1990; Cochran-Smith, Garfield, & Greenberger, 1992) as a site where such integrative learning can take place. The student teaching experience also is a place where teacher education students can influence the practice of experienced teachers. After all, student teachers come to their placements with their own knowledge and experience and potentially have something to teach their supervising teachers. In other words, learning in and from student teaching can be bidirectional (Tatel, 1996).

This study describes knowledge of educational technology as it is acquired, used and shared between student teachers and the experienced teachers with whom they work during their student teaching experience. The central questions addressed are: "What is the nature of educational technology knowledge" and "How is knowledge about teaching with technology acquired, used, and shared by student and experienced teacher pairs?" By understanding knowledge of educational technology and its development in classroom teaching and learning contexts, we hope to speak to issues of teacher preparation and development as they relate to the use of educational technology.

What is Teacher Knowledge?

Fenstermacher (1994) has noted that knowledge is a complex and often ill-defined construct in educational research. In defining "knowledge" for the purposes of this paper, we hold that teacher knowledge of educational technology is complex (Carter, 1990; Clandinin & Connelly, 1996; Cochran-Smith & Lytle, 1999; Connelly & Clandinin, 1995; Fenstermacher, 1994), situated (Greeno, 1998; Putnam & Borko, 2000) and multifaceted (Shulman, 1987).

A goal of this study is to describe the knowledge held by the participants in a way that addresses the inherent complexity and situated nature of knowledge. To do this, we frame our conception around Shulman's (1987) general framework for teacher knowledge. Previous scholarship (Margerum-Leys, 1999), has described this framework as potentially useful for describing teachers' knowledge of educational technology. When teachers' knowledge from all sources is considered as a whole, Shulman (1987) suggests that it has the following components: Content knowledge, general pedagogical knowledge, curriculum knowledge, pedagogical content knowledge, knowledge of learners and their characteristics, knowledge of educational contexts, and knowledge of educational ends, purposes, and values (p. 8). For purposes of this study, we distinguish between three types of educational technology knowledge:

- *Content knowledge* of educational technology refers to knowledge of the existence, components and capabilities of various technologies as they are used in teaching and learning settings. This might include an understanding that a range of tools exist for a particular task, the ability to choose a tool based on its fitness, and knowledge of strategies for using the tool's affordances.
- *Pedagogical knowledge* as we use the term here refers to knowledge of general pedagogical strategies and the ability to apply those strategies to the use of technology. For example, a teacher's ability to use her attendance-taking system to manage a set of word processors is an instantiation of general pedagogical knowledge within the realm of technology use.
- *Pedagogical content knowledge* of educational technology is an emerging construct. As used in this paper, it is knowledge which arises from

experience with using technology for teaching and learning and which in turn applies to the use of technology for teaching and learning. Such knowledge is specialized; it does not come from nor does it necessarily apply to other areas of teaching and learning.

Grossman (1990), in a work which follows Shulman, compresses these seven to four larger categories: subject matter knowledge (of which content knowledge is a leading component), general pedagogical knowledge, pedagogical content knowledge, and knowledge of context. Three of these—content knowledge, pedagogical knowledge, and pedagogical content knowledge—are explored at length in this paper. Although no complete studies of educational technology knowledge of which we are aware use this interpretation of the model, Fishman, Marx, Best, & Tal (in press) proposes them as the appropriate categories in his work. In choosing to focus on these particular components, we apply a portion of Shulman's model in a way that is consistent with teacher education research, though it is unusual in educational technology research.

METHODS

This paper is the direct result of using components of Shulman's model as a lens for data collection, then applying the model to the coding and results-writing process to show instances from the data that best illustrated the model in action. The methods employed in data collection and analysis were in service of this larger goal.

In designing the study, we have drawn on case study methods suggested by Yin (1984/1989, 1993) and data collection methods advocated by Emerson, Fretz and Shaw (1995), and Bogdan and Biklen (1992). The design elements are focused on the creation of a set of cases that provide a rich descriptive basis for answering the study questions. Yin describes case study research as appropriate in describing phenomena; the current case study describes the phenomenon which lies at the intersection of the rise of technology use in teaching, the need for qualified new teachers, and a developing understanding of the situated (Greeno, 1998) and complex (Shulman, 1987) nature of teacher knowledge.

Participants

Yin (1993) speaks of case study participants as being selected purposively, as representing aspects of phenomena. The participants and setting of this study serve the purpose of illuminating the intersection between the rise of technology and the need for new teachers with its accompanying emphasis on the importance of teacher preparation.

Participants for this study were selected based on technology access criteria and on accessibility to the authors. Six participants—three experienced classroom teachers and their student teachers—were approached to participate in the study, based on their placement at the research site described below. All six agreed to participate. The three experienced teachers (two female, one male) each had a minimum of seven years of classroom experience and three years of experience with student teachers. The three student teachers (two female, one male) ranged in age from 23 to 33. All were part of a graduate level year-long, interdisciplinary, cohort-based program, which combines an extended student teacher experience with the coursework necessary for a Master of Arts in education degree and secondary teaching certification. Two of the student teacher/experienced teacher pairs taught middle school science, while the remaining pair taught middle school language arts. All of the participants were known to the primary study author through his work with their student teaching program, though none of the student teacher participants was under his direct supervision.

The student teachers were part of a cohort of 30 students taking part in a year-long Master of Arts and teacher certification program. Their student teaching placements were stable throughout the academic year. In the fall semester, participants were present in their field placements two days per week. With the beginning of the second semester, the student teachers were responsible for an increasing teaching load and were present whenever school was in session.

The Research Setting

Monroe Middle School (a pseudonym, as are all of the people and place names used in this paper) was located in a lower middle class and working poor area of a blue-collar suburb of a large industrial Midwest city. The two largest demographic groups were White (79%) and African American (15%), compared to 1999 U.S. Census Bureau nationwide approximations of 76% and 11% respectively. Of the 769 students at Monroe, 233 (30.3%) were eligible for free lunch. Working class near-poverty was the norm at Monroe. Signs of low income (poor dental care, insufficient warm clothing) were common, though not ubiquitous, in the setting.

In areas other than technology, the school site was somewhat run-down, but clean and reasonably well kept. Technologically, the school was somewhat better equipped than other schools in the district and area, but not so much so as to be greatly discrepant. Each classroom had a desktop computer, which was connected to a school-wide network and to the Internet. The school also had two 30-station computer labs, one of which was Internet connected, available to classroom teachers and their students. Other technology was also available: There was a classroom set of laptop word processors, several laser disc players on mobile carts, and a fiber optic flexible video camera for each science classroom.

Pair one (Vogel and Andress, the language arts teachers) made use of portable word processors several times throughout the study. These machines, called AlphaSmarts, are roughly the size of two paperback books laid end to end. AlphaSmarts have small liquid crystal display screens, which are capable of showing approximately four lines of text at a time. Monroe Middle School owned two classroom sets of AlphaSmarts, which traveled on a rolling cart. School-wide, they were primarily used by the Language Arts classes, though they were available to other teachers. During the data observation period of this study, only pair one (the Language Arts teachers) used the AlphaSmarts. In interviews, the only participant outside of pair one who commented on the AlphaSmarts was Lloyd, who recalled having used them the previous school year.

Both pairs of science teachers made use of FlexCams to help students create presentations for their science labs. A FlexCam consisted of a video camera head on a flexible fiber optic stalk. The camera could be aimed at a lab bench, with the components of the lab visible on a large television monitor. By using the FlexCam, students could project a lab, allowing them to show it to the rest of the class; FlexCam demonstrations could also be captured on videotape for later display.

Data Sources

Two main sources comprise the data for this study: Field notes from classroom observations and teacher conversations, and transcripts from semi-structured interviews.

Field notes were collected over a 12-week period from March 1 to June 21, 1999. Classroom observations began with a 2-week data-collection instrument development period. An iterative process produced a database that served as a collection space for field notes as well as a framework for the observations. A journal that served as a meta-space for researcher observations and further note taking was also created. The database and journal were structured by considering both the classroom setting and the conceptual underpinnings of the study.

Margerum-Leys conducted all of the classroom observations and was present at the research site every school day. Classroom observations and teacher conversations yielded more than 200 entries into the field notes database, with each entry relating to a class period of classroom observation or a researcher-participant conversation. At the close of each research day, Margerum-Leys created a journal entry that served as an overview of the day's research activities. Journal entries were cross-referenced with the field notes database by numbered reference to field note database entries.

Concurrent with the classroom observations, a series of three interviews was held with each participant. Structure for the interviews was organized with guidance from Seidman's (1991) model for conducting ethnographic interviews, with the interview structure determined in part by themes identified in the classroom observations. Briefly, the three interviews concerned (a) background information, initial knowledge and beliefs (b) reflection by each participant on a specific use of technology observed in the field notes, and (c) reflection on the twelve-week data collection period. Interviews were held in the participants' classrooms to aid in recall and for convenience. Interviews were held separately and privately to encourage candor and prevent the perception that the research effort was part of the student teaching experience.

The first and third interviews were similar for all participants. While the interviews were semi-structured, allowing the participants to determine to some extent the content and character of the interview, care was taken to retain a similar structure for all participants, in order to allow comparisons to be drawn. The second interview took a different form. Each pair of participants was engaged in a conversation about a particular type of technology that had been used in that pair's classroom practice. In these second interviews, themes from the field notes were used to determine the prompts for each pair of participants. The same protocol was used for both members of the pairs, but this protocol differed from that used with the other pairs.

Figure 8.1 gives an overview of the time line of the study, including interview and data collection dates.

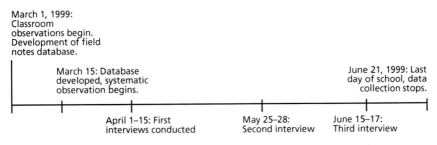

Figure 8.1.   Progress of data collection.

The data set which resulted from the field notes and interviews transcripts was quite large. Table 8.1 shows the distribution of data in the set.

Table 8.1.   Components of Data Set

Item Type	Number
Classroom observations	149
Prep period and planning sessions	35
Conversations with teachers	26
First interview lines (average)	3565 (509)
Second interview lines (average)	4272 (610)
Third interview lines (average)	3848 (550)

Analysis

Analysis was accomplished using QSR NUD*IST (an acronym standing for Nonnumerical Unstructured Data by Indexing, Searching and Theorizing), a standard qualitative data analysis tool. NUD*IST is a database tool which is capable of coding and searching very large sets of text-based data. Over the course of the 3-month observation period, a large amount of field note and transcript data was generated. These data were coded along a number of axes. Some of the codes used were descriptive in an objective sense; who was present, what type of technology was being used, where the observation took place. Other coding was more inferential; what type of knowledge (content knowledge, pedagogical knowledge, pedagogical content knowledge) was displayed, what knowledge acquisition was demonstrated by the participant, what the affordances of the technology were for the teachers and the student. To bring these descriptive and inferential codes together in a meaningful way that reduced the data for reporting, we conducted nearly 100 searches of the data set, each of which brought together one or more of the descriptive codes with one or more of the inferential codes. As a result of these searches, we were able to identify areas in the data that illustrated sections of the model particularly well.

RESULTS AND DISCUSSION

To open the results we numerically depict the profile of the data set by reporting the counts and distribution of various codes. Our purpose in doing so is to give the reader a sense of the contours of the data set. Table 8.2 shows a summary of the observation and interview coding, which formed the bulk of the data set. Because much of the data contained information about more than one person, the number of records and text units for the individual participants when added is greater than the number of records and text units for the pair. In addition, because a few records contained data that did not pertain directly to the participants (e.g., interactions with school lab personnel), the total number of field note entries is slightly greater than the sum of entries for the participants.

Table 8.2. Summary of Field Note and Interview Data

	Field notes		Interviews	
	Number	Paragraphs	Number	Lines
Andress	60	1809	3	1961
Vogel	56	1534	3	1828
Pair One	**75**	**2086**	**6**	**3789**
Brewer	46	1565	3	1758
Xie	49	1627	3	1845
Pair Two	**58**	**1906**	**6**	**3603**
Lloyd	44	1394	3	2186
Johnson	48	1399	3	2387
Pair Three	**60**	**1712**	**6**	**4573**
Total	**199**	**5847**	**18**	**11965**

One important characteristic of the data set is that the text of the observation field notes was "chunked" differently than the text of the interview transcripts. As the observer, the primary author was able to break the field notes into paragraphs as he saw fit to achieve clarity. Therefore, in the field notes a text unit is a paragraph of text. In the interviews, it was less clear how the participants would have broken their responses into paragraphs. In some cases, the responses were quite long and covered a number of themes; it is in the nature of oral discourse that paragraphs are not clearly delineated. Therefore, the interview transcripts were broken down by line to allow them to be drawn out from the much larger stream of text that generally constituted a response to an interview question. For that reason, a text unit in the interviews was a line of text (up to 80 characters) rather than a paragraph.

In the tables that follow, we report the distribution of coding along several axes. When interpreting these numbers, the reader should keep in mind that the object of this study was a descriptive report, not an argument as to which participant or pair held "more" knowledge. Counts of various categories of data are useful in envisioning how much of the data was captured by various codes, but these counts should not be misconstrued as a judgment of the quality or necessarily even the amount of knowledge held.

Coding Along the Lines of Shulman's Model

In creating this section of the study, we analyzed the data along lines directed by components of Shulman's model for teacher knowledge. The narratives which form the bulk of this chapter were built by examining the lattice formed by parsing the data by individual, by pair, and by role (mentor or student teacher) crossed with coding according to inferences made regarding teachers' content knowledge, pedagogical knowledge, and pedagogical content knowledge of educational technology.

Because this study sought to capture knowledge of educational technology, coding of content knowledge (CK), pedagogical knowledge (PK), and pedagogical content knowledge (PCK) was restricted to instances in which the teachers were using or guiding the use of educational technology for teaching and learning purposes. Not all of the field notes were of observations in which technology use was present, though when scheduling and conducting observations we prioritized opportunities to watch technology use. Additionally, some of the field notes contain descriptions of student activities or other non-teacher-centered data. These data were crucial for providing context for inferences regarding knowledge and for writing the narratives that comprise the results. However, sections of the field notes not directly related to the teacher and some use of technology for teaching and learning were not coded CK, PK, or PCK. On the positive side, having data in which teachers taught without the use of technology helped us to write the narrative sections of the paper. On the negative, coding for CK, PK, and PCK accounted for a smaller percentage of the data set than would have been the case had all parts of all field notes related specifically to educational technology use focused exclusively on the teacher.

Table 8.3 shows the division of coding for the knowledge categories for each participant, as well as for the pairs. The counts cited refer to text units in both observations and interviews. The percentage figures shown at the bottom of the table represent the fraction of the total text units (17,812) contained in all field notes and interviews.

Table 8.3.   Coding by Content, Pedagogical, and Pedagogical Content Knowledge

	Content Knowledge	Pedagogical Knowledge	Pedagogical Content Knowledge
Andress	581	860	192
Vogel	712	693	331
Pair One	**1115**	**1401**	**463**
Brewer	325	804	192
Xie	855	414	465
Pair Two	**1058**	**1050**	**633**
Lloyd	600	868	262
Johnson	936	1147	269
Pair Three	**1290**	**1886**	**405**
Total	**3463**	**4337**	**1501**
Percent Coded	**19%**	**24%**	**8%**

For the participants, content and general pedagogical knowledge were basic elements of teaching practice. The figures above are an indication that evidence of these first two facets of knowledge can be found throughout an observational data set such as the one generated by this study. The content knowledge evidenced in these observations formed the basis for decisions teachers made regarding potential tools for use in classrooms, served as foundational knowledge required to help students deal with technological hurdles, and allowed teachers to use tools in their own professional practice. To choose a few examples from many, each instance in which a teacher remembered the address of a web page, knew which menu to direct a student to, or recalled how to connect equipment so that it operated properly was an instance in which the teacher evidenced content knowledge of educational technology.

General pedagogical knowledge was equally foundational and equally prevalent. Throughout the course of the study, both student and mentor teachers drew on pedagogical knowledge acquired through non-technological teaching experiences. By the study's definition, pedagogical knowledge, which came from outside the realm of technology use and was applied to teaching with technology, was coded as general pedagogical knowledge. Integration of technology into the curriculum meant the use of technological tools to further participants' content and other student learning goals. These goals in turn were derived for the most part from more general sources than teaching about technology. Participants were teaching with technology, not necessarily about technology. Unsurprisingly, integration of learning goals into the mainstream of curriculum was mirrored by integration of teaching strategies from the mainstream of pedagogy. When teachers made choices regarding pedagogical strategies, they frequently employed general pedagogical knowledge, which accounts for the frequency with which this code was found in the data set.

Pedagogical content knowledge was less frequently in evidence, for reasons both definitional and empirical. By definition, we restricted pedagogical content knowledge to strategies arising from and applicable to the use of technology in teaching and learning. Because that definition was narrower than the definition for general pedagogical knowledge (the application of general pedagogical principles to teaching with technology), it was natural that PCK appeared less frequently than pedagogical knowledge.

The extra layer of complexity inherent in teaching with technology, along with the realities of middle school teaching, contributed to the low incidence of PCK of technology within this data set. Participants did adjust their instruction to address challenges, which arose, acquiring PCK in the process. In the busyness of working with both students and technology, though, this was an incremental process. Teacher planning time was limited and rarely focused on consideration of issues related to teaching with technology. Development of PCK of technology, both by definition and by the exigencies of the professional lives of the participants, occurred in the context of teaching practice and was pressed by the complication of managing a classroom of students along with one or many technological tools. Still, PCK did develop for the participants in this study and over the course of the three months, there was a heartening accumulation of incidences for study.

Reporting of the Results: Narrative Explorations of Shulman's Model

In this, the main subsection of the results, we present a series of narratives. Each of these is designed to illuminate a facet of teacher knowledge of educational technology as viewed through Shulman's model of teacher knowledge. As has been referred to previously, we focus on educational technology rather than subject area knowledge for descriptive purposes. We recognize that educational technology knowledge is brought to bear in service of subject area domain teaching and learning. However, that is not the focus of this paper; here, we concentrate on technology. Our goal in doing so is empirical, to assist the reader in understanding the participants' approach to educational technology in particular.

For each teacher as well as for teachers as a group, teacher knowledge is an evolving body. As educational priorities develop and change, the knowledge required to fulfill the role of "teacher" evolves. Individual teachers acquire knowledge from their settings, their practices, the materials they use, and the people around them. Knowledge, in the case of the participants of this study, flows from mentor teachers to students, from student teachers to mentors, and forms a cycle of student teacher–mentor teacher–subsequent teachers. Following the three major chapter sections that use Shulman's model to describe educational technology knowledge, we include a section on knowledge acquisition and flow that addresses this cycle.

Content Knowledge of Educational Technology: Current Ideas from Student Teachers, Specific Applications from Their Mentors

Content knowledge is the most basic of the knowledge types discussed here. It is the "what to teach" of whatever domain is being conveyed. For purposes of this study, content knowledge of educational technology was defined as knowledge regarding the existence and capabilities of various technologies for teacher and student use. Content knowledge included knowing which software would be appropriate for a particular teaching and learning task and how to use that software. For example, the student teachers had seen a variety of web sites as part of their preparatory coursework. Their content knowledge included knowing the addresses of particular web sites and being familiar with the pages on those sites. Branching out from that example, content knowledge more broadly included knowledge of the capabilities of a web browser and knowledge of how to transfer text and pictures from the Web to a word processing document for the purposes of note taking. In all three pairs of student teachers and mentor teachers, content knowledge of educational technology flowed in both directions (mentor teacher to student teacher and student teacher to mentor teacher), though the kinds of content knowledge each participant brought to the setting differed.

The three student teachers brought with them a relatively broad range of knowledge of technology, especially of applications that were generally used for personal productivity. All of the student teachers were proficient and regular e-mail users; all were able to find information using search engines on the World Wide Web; all used word processing software to create documents for their own personal and professional uses.

In the third interview, Brewer (the mentor teacher in pair 2) indicated that observing his student teacher was an effective way to acquire content knowledge. In a passage from the third interview, Brewer had this to say about acquiring content knowledge from Xie.

> He's absolutely helped me in some ways, but I've learned I think, probably I've learned from him better by, instead of saying "teach me how to do this," my better approach is to say "okay, would you start doing this and I'm going

to watch over your shoulder." And he explains it to me no problem. (Brewer, Third Interview)

In crediting his student teacher with helping him to acquire content knowledge, Brewer also drew a distinction between the immediacy of access to the student teacher and the relatively removed nature of traditional in-service programs:

> I've usually found that in in-services, seldom are you able to walk out of it and incorporate it immediately. You know, usually it takes me a while to digest, "All right, what is it that you learned. How can I use this now?" It's not as yielding. You've got to figure out, "Okay, now here's the technology, here's how you use the technology," now you've got to bring your personality around to be able to use it and use it comfortably. (Brewer, Third Interview)

Xie, Brewer's student teacher, had a similar view of the exchange of educational technology knowledge between the two of them. In the third interview, he characterized their relationship in terms of educational technology knowledge as follows:

> Most of the stuff is he'll bring up an idea. And then, what I'll do is I will take the initiative to sit down and play with things. And maybe show him, like what I show him is more of what the programs can do. And he'll say, "Maybe we can do a computer lab simulation here." And I'll sit down and go through the lab and find out what the limitations are, what things need to be highlighted, and I'll come back and say "you know what, this is a great lab, but we need to make sure that we tell the kids about this and this and this and this." And so otherwise they may be misled or may not get the results that they want.
>
> **Margerum-Leys:** What kinds of changes does he make [in instantiating the lesson]? What differences do you see?
>
> **Xie:** [long pause] I think that what he does is, I think he's a little better with relating information and concepts to the younger crowd than I am. In a more entertaining and fun way. So he'll do that, he'll add that into it. That's something that I'm still working on. I'm having a hard time, I'm getting a little tired, but I'm just, I'm not accustomed to this age group. So, but I think that he takes what, the information that I've given him and manipulates it in a way that younger minds can grasp it quicker. (Xie, Third Interview)

In this example, notice that Xie shifted from considering content knowledge, which both he and Brewer considered Xie to be a source of, to considering pedagogical knowledge. The passage hinted that Brewer was a source of this knowledge, basing appropriate classroom adaptations on the content knowledge provided by Xie and infusing it with the knowledge needed to instantiate it in the classroom.

Content Knowledge Flows from Student Teacher to Mentor Teacher

In the opening example above, student teachers were sources of content knowledge for their mentor teachers. The mentor teachers recognized and valued the content knowledge of the student teachers, comparing it favorably with other sources of content knowledge. The episode below illustrated this phenomenon by giving a more complete portrayal of a specific instance in which content knowledge held by a student teacher was shared with her mentor teacher.

For each pair of participants, we selected one classroom use of technology to be the focus of the second interview. In the case of Johnson and Lloyd, their use of a virtual tour of a plant cell was the selected use of technology. The criteria for focusing on this use of technology were that (a) it took place in the time frame in which the second interview was scheduled, (b) technology was used by students for learning, and (c) the use demonstrated teacher knowledge of educational technology.

As a result of focusing on the virtual cell activity for interviews with two participants in addition to the seven field note entries from the activity, we had a large amount of data from which to work. The particular incident below was selected because the data available included both observations and commentary from the participants in the form of interview data. The notes and participant perspective came together well to provide a description of content knowledge in the setting which was representative of the best of what happened at Monroe Middle School as well as illustrating part of Shulman's model.

During her science methods class, Johnson (the student teacher in pair three) had been exposed to a variety of web sites. These sites were found and shared among the methods students in connection with a class assignment. On day 42 of the study, Johnson implemented a lesson in which she had her students explore one of these sites.

The Web site allowed students to view images of a plant cell as captured by optical and electron microscopes. Students could manipulate the cell as if they were dissecting it with a scalpel. Parts of the cell were labeled, with text on the web site explaining the functions of the various cell components.

In planning the activity, Johnson used the word processor on her laptop computer to create a worksheet to accompany the web site. On this sheet, she asked students relatively low-level questions such as fill-in-the-blank definitions. She also asked higher level questions: In one section, she asked students to draw what they saw on screen and tell her what the part of the cell reminded them of.

Lloyd (Johnson's mentor teacher) took a less active role in the planning. In the days prior to students' exploration of the web site, she had viewed the web site. While Johnson was responsible for the planning of the activity and the creation of the accompanying materials, Lloyd conferred with her during their planning period and was aware of the steps being taken by Johnson.

Implementation of the activity went smoothly: Students seemed engaged in exploring the web site and completing the assigned worksheet. Aside from occasional crashes caused by the computers' web caches over-flowing, there were no technology failures and no instances of students straying from the web site either intentionally or unintentionally. From a content knowledge standpoint, this lack of technological difficulty may be important, as is discussed below.

Johnson evidenced considerable content knowledge about the web site being used by the students. At the beginning of each period, she spent a few minutes defining terms used on the site. Having explored the site thoroughly, she was familiar with the science vocabulary that students would encounter. As an anticipatory activity, she projected various images from the site onto the projection system used in the computer lab. Her smooth navigation of the site demonstrated her content knowledge of the site's structure, as well as her content knowledge of the use of a web browser.

After watching Johnson implement this activity in three consecutive classes, Lloyd taught the same lesson plan. Her implementation was very much like Johnson's: Each spent approximately the first 20 minutes of a 50-minute period giving directions and showing the site on the computer projection system. Following this introductory session, students worked in pairs for the remaining 30 minutes of the period, browsing the web site, viewing on line slides, and completing the worksheet.

In the second interview, Lloyd had this to say about the activity:

Margerum-Leys: If you were going to tell [another teacher] how to enact this lab, what would you tell that person?

Lloyd: I'll say "you've gotta do this!" I don't think they need a whole, whole lot [of technology knowledge]. I mean, it just depends on how they are technology wise and the lab people can do that. I'd tell them about the fact that after a few hours we found that we had to restart. Because we started having the crashes. So that's a management issue. [...]

So I think really once the legwork is done on it, it's really pretty, a simple thing to do. Just do it. I'd say, "Do it." [laughs]. "Don't skip this one, this is fun." (Lloyd, Second Interview)

From Johnson, Lloyd had gained content knowledge regarding the existence of this site. By watching Johnson teach the lesson, she gained knowledge of the site's structure. Lloyd also gained pedagogical knowledge from watching Johnson. Her implementation was very similar to Johnson's, indicating that she had acquired the pedagogical knowledge required to teach the lesson by being exposed to Johnson's classroom practice. Content knowledge forms a base on which to build pedagogical knowledge—without knowledge of the existence and structure of the virtual cell activity, Johnson could not have implemented it and Lloyd could not have picked it up from her.

Content Knowledge Flows from Mentor Teacher to Student Teacher

The following event is representative of an interesting phenomenon—student teachers learning about a technology in use at their school setting but not encountered in their own previous technology use. Of the 11 instances in which a student teacher gained this type of content knowledge of technology from a mentor teacher, this event was typical in that the student teacher learned about a type of technology in use in the school setting that the student teacher had not encountered in her personal use of technology. We selected this event because it was drawn from interview data and thus we were able to get the participant perspective as confirmation of the observational inference regarding knowledge acquisition.

During the first interview as well as a teacher conversation recorded in the field notes, Johnson commented that Lloyd had helped her learn about the use of laser disks. Margerum-Leys subsequently observed both participants using laser disks to help them engage students in classroom discussions and to show photographs and video illustrating science concepts. When asked about the role that Lloyd had played in her use of educational technology, Johnson cited learning about "laser disks, using videos in the classroom, and the FlexCam" (Johnson, First Interview). To Johnson, the laser disk was a "new" technology of which she had no content knowledge. For Lloyd, this was a system which she had learned about through her classroom practice and about which she had considerable content knowledge. She demonstrated this knowledge by leading classroom activities in which she found clips on the laser disk, operating it smoothly in support of classroom discussion and inquiry. From observing Lloyd and exploring the laser disk on her own, Johnson acquired knowledge of the technology's capacities and operation and made its use part of her own teaching practice.

The mentor teachers who participated in this study held content knowledge that allowed them to use technology in their teaching as well as in their professional and personal pursuits. In certain instances, mentor teachers held content knowledge that was functional in the particular setting. While the student teachers had been at the university or in the business world for the previous five years, the teachers had been working in their classrooms. In terms of technologies in use *for teaching in their particular setting*, the mentor teachers were therefore more "up to date" than their student teachers. Laser disks, even when they were current state-of-the-art technology, were primarily used in K–12 settings. Johnson would have been unlikely to be exposed to their use in her experience in the business world, even though she used other technologies in her work. Content knowledge of educational technology can spring from areas outside of education, but practicing teachers may hold content knowledge of applications of which their student teachers are unaware, despite the student teacher being generally conversant in technology's use.

The Role of Content Knowledge

Content knowledge of educational technology serves at least two broad purposes: To allow teachers to envision instances in which technology might be appropriately used in their teaching and to allow them to instantiate those visions. Content knowledge is the basis on which all other knowledge is built. Without content knowledge, teachers' options are limited and their applications narrowed.

Conversation in interviews and observations of participants indicated that in general, student teachers were knowledgeable regarding personal productivity software and current technologies. However, mentor teachers' knowledge of technologies in use at their site in some instances gave them a benefit in using technology in their teaching. This reveals an important distinction: The content knowledge required for teaching and learning can be different from that which allows teachers to accomplish personal tasks. There is a danger in assuming that student teachers who know a lot about technology as used in their everyday lives will have the content knowledge needed to be successful in their teaching roles.

There were relatively few technological malfunctions associated with participants' use of educational technology. During web activities which we observed in the mid-1990s, computer crashes were commonplace, occurring several times per class period. Internet connection problems were also frequent. In order to keep activities running, teachers needed content knowledge to allow them to successfully troubleshoot technological problems, which if left unsolved would have brought their intended activity to a halt. For the episodes recounted above, such content knowledge became secondary. The participants, for example, knew how to prevent web browser crashes by quitting and restarting the browser software. Otherwise, the software and hardware were robust enough that participants did not have to worry about them failing. They could concentrate on science content and web navigation skills as the necessary and sufficient content knowledge base. In the early days of technology use in education, teachers needed to be well versed in solving technological difficulties. With more stable technology, as typified by the event above, the content knowledge of the technology faded somewhat into the background, allowing more student-centered concerns to be foregrounded.

Pedagogical Knowledge of Educational Technology

Pedagogical knowledge of educational technology, as the phrase is used in this study, involves understanding how general pedagogical strategies apply to the use of technology. Practicing teachers have a store of pedagogical knowledge which they have acquired through their teaching practice as well as through conversations with knowledgeable others and through other sources. When faced with a new situation, existing pedagogical knowledge may come into play, even when the content context is different from the content context present at the time the pedagogical knowledge was initially acquired. In educational technology, pedagogical strategies relevant to teaching in general may be applied when using technology. The knowledge itself does not arise from technology-enhanced teaching experience, but it can be applied to situations in which technology is being used in teaching and learning. The narrative below illustrates one such occasion.

Bringing Together Attendance and Hardware Management

This episode incorporates three phenomena of interest: Pedagogical knowledge drawn from non-technological teaching experience, knowledge acquired by the student teacher from the mentor teacher, and knowledge enhanced by participants' repeated practice.

During the first occasion on which Margerum-Leys observed the AlphaSmarts in use by this pair's students, Andress used a simple but effective strategy for managing the classroom set of AlphaSmarts. As she took attendance, Andress assigned numbers to her students. These numbers were the numbers in her grade-keeping file on the computer. The slots in the cart full of AlphaSmarts had corresponding numbers. After she had taken attendance and assigned numbers, she had students come up in groups of five by student number to pick up the AlphaSmart with the same number.

This strategy achieved two purposes. First, by establishing a consistent one-to-one correspondence between students and machines, Andress was able to easily keep track of which student was responsible for which AlphaSmart. Second, once the numbers were assigned, Andress had a means by which to limit the number of students who were at the cart at any particular time.

When she first used the AlphaSmarts, Vogel (the student teacher in pair one) did not use the same strategy. In the interview about their use of the AlphaSmarts, she remarked:

Vogel: Mostly what I learned is like how to hand them [the AlphaSmarts] out and how to collect them. Honest to God that was about the biggest thing I learned [laughs]. I think the first time I sort of just said, "Okay go get your AlphaSmarts." And it was like mass herding to the little cabinet. And again, I didn't learn my lesson then and I said, "Okay, well, put your AlphaSmarts away." And mass herding.

Jon: So did that change over the course of the day? The way you handed them out?

Vogel: Absolutely. [laughs] . . . I mean I learned by watching [Andress]. I'll be perfectly honest about that one. (Vogel, Second Interview)

In observing differences between Vogel and Andress, Andress' simple technique for managing the AlphaSmarts had distinct advantages. After trying to regulate students taking out and returning the AlphaSmarts without using a numbering system, Vogel noticed Andress' approach and was able to improve her own instructional management.

Once content knowledge is established, pedagogical knowledge needs to be acquired and brought to bear in order for teachers to be effective users of technology in their teaching practice. Pedagogical knowledge can be addressed in university coursework from a theoretical standpoint. As tools and technologies are introduced to students, teacher educators have an obligation to place the use of those tools within a teaching and learning context. However, pedagogical knowledge can be difficult to impart through learning experiences that are not embedded in a classroom setting. The account above illustrates an example of a simple strategy that improved instructional management. The strategy was acquired by the student teacher after she had tried to manage the technology without it. Observation of her mentor teacher allowed her to see a different approach; access to teaching opportunities allowed her to instantiate this approach, making it a part of her own practice. Additionally, Vogel benefitted from the opportunity to both watch and direct multiple iterations of the same lesson. Her comments in the interview indicate that she sees the value of observing and teaching the same lesson more than once to different groups of students. This is a benefit, which is only available in the context of classroom practice and cannot be easily achieved in the context of university coursework.

We do not mean to overstate the importance of the example above. It is, after all, a simple strategy for dealing with a common problem. However, it points up the importance of pedagogical knowledge in using technology and the value of acquiring pedagogical knowledge within the student teaching setting.

Pedagogical Content Knowledge (PCK) Of Educational Technology:
An Emerging Knowledge Set Unique to Teaching with Technology

Of the three types of knowledge addressed in this study, Pedagogical Content Knowledge, or PCK, is the most difficult to define. While PCK has become a "cottage industry" (Fenstermacher, 1994) in educational research, few field-based studies of which we are aware address PCK as it relates to educational technology knowledge. PCK of educational technology is defined here as understandings for teaching with technology which arise from knowledge of technology as it is applied in classroom settings. PCK of educational technology does not derive from, nor does it necessarily apply to, teaching without educational technology. As such, it is unique to the use of educational technology. In the sections below, we describe examples of Pedagogical Content Knowledge as observed and commented on among the teaching pairs.

A Strategy for Using Video to Demonstrate a Science Lab

This first episode illustrates a simple technique for improving students' use of a piece of equipment. As with the pedagogical knowledge event cited above, a simple example when unpacked reveals an interesting fragment of pedagogical content knowledge as well as an illustration of how such knowledge is acquired and shared. The simplicity and ease of implementation of the strategy below make it interesting conceptually as well— knowledge need not be complex to be useful and need not be earthshaking to be conceptually fulfilling.

Another reason for selecting this event for reporting is that it illustrates how knowledge can be shared across classrooms. Once Xie had created the strategy reported below, it was used by both student and mentor teachers in both of the science pairs. At this site, it was unusual for teachers to share knowledge across classrooms. While the teachers taught in teams and some knowledge was shared during team meetings, at no time during the study period did a teacher observe another teacher in a classroom setting, other than mentor teachers' observations of their own student teachers and vice versa. The example below was selected in part because sharing of knowledge across classrooms was an unusual occurrence.

On day ten of the data collection, Margerum-Leys observed Xie (the student teacher in pair two) using masking tape to create a rectangle on the top of the lab bench. When asked to talk about what he was doing, Xie explained that the masking tape represented the outside border of what was visible on the television monitor when using the FlexCam. Xie had noticed that it was difficult for students to monitor the visibility of items on the lab bench while they were performing their demonstration. To aid students in using the FlexCam, Xie came up with the strategy of creating the tape border.

Observations of students using the FlexCam indicated that having the border set out on the table helped them to keep their demonstration in view on the television monitor. Using the FlexCam, performing the required science lab, and explaining the process to the class was a complex undertaking. Having a strategy to make the camera use easier was simple but not trivial for the students.

A few days after Xie implemented this strategy, Lloyd (the mentor teacher in pair three) used the FlexCam in her classroom. Margerum-Leys mentioned to her that Xie had recently used the FlexCam for the same purpose and that he had created a strategy for its use. During her planning period, Xie showed her how to set up the tape border on her lab bench. Subsequently, all of the science teachers used this strategy when using the FlexCam.

Adding a tape border to a lab bench to aid students in using video is a simple innovation. Realizing it was necessary and creating the innovation is an instance of pedagogical content knowledge gained through classroom practice. The knowledge arose from teaching with technology and was applicable to teaching with technology. It was an understanding of technology that was interwoven with the perspective of teaching and learning—a different understanding than might be reached by a non-teaching technician. This different understanding is a classic hallmark of PCK. It is knowledge in service of teaching, generated through and used for teaching practice. Once the knowledge is present in the setting, it can be shared by teachers in the context of their practice as part of the formal or informal planning process.

The knowledge itself—place a tape frame on the table to show the field of view for the video monitor—in this instance could be easily imparted through university coursework. Seeing the instructional need for the strategy, developing it, and recognizing its utility are the characteristics which cause this knowledge to be considered pedagogical content knowledge.

Adapting to New Equipment

Adapting to new technology may require teachers to tailor the knowledge they already hold or to acquire new knowledge. Confronted with an unknown, teachers must decide what prior knowledge applies to the unknown technology and what new knowledge must be created. The event below describes the only instance during the study period where participants encountered an unknown piece of technology. As with the pedagogical event above, this event shows how repeated iterations of a lesson afford participants with the opportunity to acquire new knowledge and adapt their practices.

In the pedagogical knowledge example above, we briefly described AlphaSmarts and their use in the classroom. The language arts pair

(Andress/Vogel) had used AlphaSmarts on several occasions: Andress had also used the equipment during the previous year and had received in-service instruction by Monroe Middle School's computer lab coordinator in their use. On day 19, Andress and Vogel were surprised to find that the AlphaSmarts they were accustomed to using in their classroom had been replaced by upgraded models. Neither participant knew that they would have new equipment until the students were present in the room and they opened the cabinet containing the AlphaSmarts.

The lesson plan for the day was as follows: The teacher was to spend the first ten minutes of the period going over the previous day's quiz. Students' homework was to prepare a two- to three-page longhand rough draft in preparation for using the word processors. The bulk of the period was to be spent with students using the AlphaSmarts; students who had not completed their rough drafts were to do so before using the technology. Andress noted in the second interview that use of the AlphaSmarts was motivating to students and that they completed more homework in anticipation of using the technology. That was the case in this activity. Almost all students had prepared a rough draft and the turn-in rate for homework otherwise was between half and two-thirds. Throughout the periods in which students were observed using the word processors, students seemed engaged and on task.

During the first period that the pair used the new machines, the only new feature the teachers had to contend with was a relocated power switch. A moment's exploration of the new machines revealed that the power switch had been moved but that its functionality had not changed. With students in the room, Andress and Vogel could not take the time to further explore any new capabilities of the word processors. As their students used the equipment during this period, their teachers observed their progress and found that the new equipment had built-in spell-checking software. The atmosphere in the room was of co-discovery of differences in the new machines, with the students completing a writing task through the use of the technology, and Andress and Vogel watching students work, noticing any differences between previous and new equipment.

In the second period that the pair had students write with the word processors, Andress (the mentor teacher) introduced the new machines to the students. She had students walk through the spell-checking program at the end of the period. Andress directed each step and checked that students all were on the same step of the process. The use of the new feature was directed and managed closely by the teacher.

The third period saw Andress trying a different approach to the new AlphaSmarts. She pointed out to students that the machines had been updated, and then asked them to notice what the new features were. She and the students engaged in a conversation about the relocated power switch and the spell-check feature. Having a sense of the new machines and two periods of experience teaching with them, she seemed to open up into a more interactive style.

In the fourth period, Vogel (the student teacher) became the lead teacher. Her task was to enact the same lesson plan that Andress had taught in the previous three periods. In this pair, the student teacher "shadowing" the lesson prepared by the mentor teacher was the most common mode. Vogel's teaching of the writing activity was very similar to Andress'. The only observed difference was that Vogel used more class time going over the quiz—fifteen minutes as compared with ten for Andress. Vogel's classroom management style was less polished than Andress', which made her somewhat less efficient in the earlier part of the class. Andress remained in the room throughout the period, entering grades from the quizzes onto the classroom computer. Midway through the class period, Andress reminded Vogel to introduce the changes in the AlphaSmarts to the students. Vogel looked chagrined to have forgotten to mention this earlier. She mentioned the relocated power switch to students, and then asked Andress to remind her how to use the spell-check function. As Andress had taught with this equipment in the three previous periods, she was able to talk through the new function from memory. Andress, through her classroom practice, had developed the knowledge sought by Vogel.

The bustle of classroom life leaves teachers with little time to plan for the integration of new technology. Sometimes, as in this example, new technology appears in the classroom with little or no warning and with no technological support for the teacher or students. Fortunately, the particular equipment used in this example was not radically different from that to which the teachers were accustomed. Over the course of the day, the teachers learned about the capabilities of the new equipment. As they became more conversant with it, their instruction changed from co-discovery to teacher-directed to interactive with the students.

Observing these two teachers, Margerum-Leys was struck by how flexible they were. The new equipment did not throw them off course with their lesson. They quickly integrated a new function of the equipment into their lesson plan and migrated from a teacher-centered to a somewhat student-centered mode of engagement with the students.

In the university setting, the lack of classroom context might make it difficult for students to acquire knowledge of how to integrate new technology into existing curricular activities. When engaged in the field setting, these teachers adapted quickly to the change. The student teacher gained experience in becoming adaptable. She may not encounter this particular technology in her next teaching assignment, but in encountering this technology and adapting to it, she has gained valuable knowledge and experience in dealing with new equipment in the pressure cooker of the classroom.

Sources of Knowledge Regarding Technology-Infused Curriculum Materials

As mentioned in the FlexCam border example above, it was unusual for teachers to acquire knowledge from classrooms other than their own. There were no instances in which teachers (student or mentor) visited each other's classrooms while students were present. There were, however, instances in which teachers observed other teachers in the computer lab. The computer lab acted as common ground—teachers dropped in while instruction was taking place, and observers and observed seemed comfortable with the arrangement.

During the study, the science teachers at Monroe were working with a new textbook sequence that had just been purchased by the district. One component of the textbook was a CD-ROM containing virtual labs. The CD presented common science problems in a somewhat realistic on-screen lab setting. During the course of the school year, each science teacher used the CD-ROM four to six times. Topics covered included force and motion, acid rain, the Coreolis effect, and factors in plant growth, among other topics. For the most part, teachers learned about these materials through exploration. Brewer made the following comment about his exposure to the CD-ROM material:

> ...as far as implementing it, I think the most honest way was . . . I didn't do it by the book. ... I basically got on and played with the labs, just played around in it and saw what all of the bells and whistles were, and I was intrigued immediately. Then from there, I went to the resource component of the lab, basically a hardcovered book and looked at some of the questions they asked and had to weigh, "Are these valuable questions? Are these the kinds of questions that might improve learning or might get them to think?" And, I was pretty satisfied with it. (Brewer, Second Interview)

In addition to acquiring knowledge through exploration and interaction with the curriculum materials themselves, teachers in this study acquired knowledge from and shared knowledge with other teachers. On day two of the study, pair three (Johnson/Lloyd) was in the computer lab with their students. The students were working in pairs at the computers, completing a virtual lab on acid rain. Johnson and Lloyd, who almost invariably co-taught all lessons, introduced the main question for the lab and the lab equipment students would use. They then took on the role of facilitators, circulating through the room and helping individual pairs of students.

While Johnson and Lloyd were doing this, several other science teachers came into the computer lab on their planning period to see how the virtual labs were being used by students. These particular teachers had not previously been exposed to the materials themselves. In the lab on this occasion, they followed a three-step process: First, Johnson and Lloyd directed them to a computer not in use by any students. The teachers looked through the virtual lab, familiarizing themselves with the curriculum materials. Second, the teachers walked through the lab, looking over the shoulders of various students. Finally, they approached Johnson and Lloyd with questions about managing the instruction. Both Johnson and Lloyd fielded content knowledge questions (lab materials and procedures) and pedagogical content knowledge questions (student and time management during these particular labs).

At Monroe, it was unusual for teachers to visit each other's classrooms, even when no students were present. It was also unusual for teachers to meet to plan or discuss instruction. The teaching teams met: Pairs 1 and 2 were on the same team, which met weekly. These meetings centered almost entirely around student and calendar issues rather than instructional issues. The event described above, in which pair three served as a pedagogical resource for teachers, was an exception to the rule that teachers do not observe each other's instructional practices.

Lloyd and Johnson served a valuable role in the example above. They were able to introduce new materials to teachers, model instruction, and answer content and pedagogical questions. The lab setting, in which Johnson and Lloyd's students were working their way through the materials, provided a rich context for the visiting teachers.

Why was this event so unusual at this school and why, when it did occur, was it situated in the computer lab? Perhaps the lab serves as a neutral setting. Since it is no one's particular classroom, visiting teachers may feel comfortable coming into the room and teachers who are working with students may be more at ease acting as resources.

When we designed this study, we expected more occurrences of events resembling the one described above than actually occurred. The field setting is potentially a rich source of both questions and answers. Additionally, it is an environment that is difficult to describe, much less replicate, in the context of university coursework. Still, while it was an unusual event, it was a valuable one. The teachers who visited the lab setting had a realistic look at how instruction proceeded with real students interacting with real curriculum as part of their normal class work. Johnson and Lloyd had the opportunity to serve as pedagogical guides, adding to their value to the school.

A Cycle of Knowledge Acquisition

Knowledge about teaching with educational technology is evolving rapidly as both our understanding of the role of technology in teaching and technology itself changes continuously. In this research site, we observed part of this development and listened as mentor teachers commented on the larger picture of educational technology knowledge as a multi-year enterprise informed by and informing both student and mentor teachers.

Since the mentor teachers have had successive student teachers from the same program for several years, there is an opportunity for knowledge gained from student teachers to reach maturity in the classroom setting with the mentor teachers and be available for subsequent student teachers.

An Example of This Cycle

Four phenomena which were coded in the data set converge in the example below, making it a particularly rich representation of how various strands come together in the coding process of highlighting the particular events related in this chapter. The following are represented in this event: Content knowledge, acquisition of knowledge from the researcher, sharing of knowledge with student teacher, and sharing of knowledge with another mentor teacher.

On the first day of the study, Andress (the mentor teacher in pair one) was interested in customizing her record keeping software. She realized that the software's pre-loaded categories for attendance ("Absent," "Excused," or "Tardy") did not match the attendance categories used at Monroe Middle School. To bring her record keeping in line with the system used at Monroe, she needed to be able to record in-school and out-of-school suspensions, as well as field trips.

During a preparation period, Margerum-Leys showed Andress how to add the requested attendance categories. Doing so required approximately 20 minutes, during which time he provided content knowledge of the software and Andress contributed knowledge of the school setting. Andress controlled the computer, with Margerum-Leys sitting beside her. The session was more like a conversation than a tutoring session, with both participants making contributions.

After this session, Andress shared the new knowledge with Vogel, her student teacher. For the remainder of the study, the pair used the system to keep track of their daily attendance. Andress also shared the knowledge with Brewer, who served as the science teacher on her team and the mentor teacher in pair two.

But where did the software itself come from? Brewer indicated that the particular record-keeping software used on this site was introduced by a student teacher during the previous year. The student teacher, in turn, had been introduced to the software during his teacher preparation course on educational technology. This example represented a chain of events: Through his teacher education coursework, the student teacher was introduced to the software at the university and brought it to the school site. The mentor teacher used the software, but realized that it would be more useful if it could be modified for the particular setting. She acquired from a university staff member the knowledge needed to modify the configuration of the software and shared that knowledge with both other mentor teachers and her student teachers. At each step, knowledge was added, with each participant both gaining and contributing.

In this site, knowledge of educational technology was evolving. All of the mentor teachers had been involved with the teacher preparation program for several years. In each year, a student teacher brought her knowledge to the classroom and instantiated that knowledge in the setting. Mentor teachers added value in terms of pedagogical strategies and opportunities for student teachers to integrate content knowledge with their developing pedagogical knowledge.

The cycle continued as a new student teacher entered the setting. Mentor teachers had content knowledge about educational technology which has been constructed, in part, from interactions with previous student teachers. This existing knowledge of educational technology was conveyed by the mentor teachers, but in a more pedagogically appropriate form than it had been in the previous years. In turn, new technology knowledge was brought in by student teachers and shared with the mentor teachers and the cycle continued.

The role of the university teacher preparation program was important in sustaining this cycle. As the educational technologist for the program, Margerum-Leys had been able to structure students' technology preparation in part based on his own familiarity with the technological capacities in place in the field settings. Student teachers brought to their settings content knowledge that was applicable to their situations. For the past three years, Margerum-Leys had visited this and several other school sites weekly. His observations of technology applications in the field settings informed subsequent technology preparation of student teachers. The student teachers served as a pipeline for educational technology content knowledge; their practices and the practices of their mentor teachers served as a feedback loop that informed subsequent teacher preparation coursework and more importantly, subsequent student teachers' experiences in their placement.

Examples of Educational Technology Knowledge

This section of the chapter brings together the types of technology knowledge illustrated in the narratives above, along with some uncovered in the analysis but not specifically reported as part of the narratives. Our intent in creating this section is not to present a canonical list, but to display in a consolidated form the knowledge evidenced in the setting, categorizing the knowledge through the classifications used in analyzing the data. In the tables below, we order and group the knowledge examples based on their similarity to each other as observed in the field notes.

Content Knowledge

Content knowledge (CK) as defined in this study was the "what to teach" of a teacher's knowledge base. For technology, this included an awareness of potential tools, the capacities and structures of those tools, and specific techniques to use with specific tools, to name a few. Of the three components of knowledge explored in this study, content knowledge was the easiest to codify.

Table 8.4 gives examples of the categories of content knowledge brought into use by teachers in the research setting. An important distinction between the examples listed here as CK and those listed below as PCK is that these examples were of the kinds of understandings which might be reached by anyone encountering the tools used by the participants.

Table 8.4.   Examples of Content Knowledge

Participants had content knowledge of:
The existence of a variety of tools
Hardware controls
Hardware capabilities
Configuration of hardware and software
Likely equipment failures
Troubleshooting equipment
Sequences of directions found within software-based structured lessons
Interfaces within software tools
Security features
File structures within storage space available at the site
Decoding web addresses for clues as to authorship
General structures of web sites
Structures of specific web sites
Content available through various software tools and web sites
Vocabulary regarding technology
Keyboarding and other data entry techniques
Material available to aid in professional networking and the job search

Pedagogical Knowledge

As used in this study, pedagogical knowledge (PK) referred to the application of general pedagogical techniques to situations in which technology was used for teaching and learning. The key distinction between the examples listed in Table 8.5 as PK and those listed in the section below as PCK are that these examples are drawn from or are applicable to general experiences teachers have had, or from resources that are not specific to the use of technology. While the knowledge examples listed below are particular to teachers and teaching, they are not particular to the use of educational technology.

Table 8.5.   Examples of Pedagogical Knowledge

Participants had pedagogical knowledge of:
Checking for understanding
Time management
Motivating students
Being able to foresee the students' perspective
Using models of student work to help other students complete the same or similar tasks
Scaffolding in the sense of knowing how much support to give and withhold
Formative assessment of student learning as a means to gauge instructional effectiveness
Adjustment of instruction to meet special needs
Effective student grouping
Ordering and limiting directions
Holding students accountable for equipment used
Assessment of student work
Self-awareness of matching strengths to student needs
Awareness of partner's strengths

Pedagogical Content Knowledge

Pedagogical Content Knowledge (PCK) was defined here as knowledge which participants held which was derived from and applicable to teaching and learning situations involving educational technology. Of the three components of knowledge explored in this study, it was the most difficult to define and to separate out for analysis. In order to qualify as PCK, knowledge had to be specific to the use of educational technology. The knowledge listed in Table 8.6 represents a special understanding of the content held by teachers, which allows them to be more effective in their instruction when using educational technology, and supporting students in using educational technology.

Table 8.6.   Examples of Pedagogical Content Knowledge

Participants had pedagogical content knowledge of:

The time required to teach about and with particular technologies

How to envision potential student problems with particular technologies and plan instruction to support students as they work through those problems

Common mistakes made by students and how to help them correct, having made the error

Interface and other technological characteristics which have similarities between pieces of software and how to help students to enact previous knowledge

Strategies for minimizing time spent learning technology v. learning content

When to explain a procedure v. model v. do the procedure for the student

The kinds of things students might do to try to cheat an instructional system and how to prevent that

Recognition of key elements of technology-infused activities, ability to adjust instruction to highlight and support those elements

Deep understanding of software interfaces, allowing the teacher to spot a student's progress and profitable next steps

Connect abstract technological experiences with concrete examples

Configuring instruction and learning tasks for a variety of technological capacities

Awareness of appropriate alternatives to use in the event of technological failure

Repurposing non-educational software for educational purposes

Adapting strategies when using educational software to allow different goals to be met than those envisioned by the software creator

Matching the sequencing of an instructional technology activity with appropriate sequencing for students given curricular goals, time constraints, and particular abilities of individual and groups of students

Configuring hardware and software to minimize errors, maximize learning

Communicating salient pedagogical points regarding applications to other educators (rare, happened only in context of computer lab, not in classroom)

LIMITATIONS AND DIRECTIONS FOR FURTHER RESEARCH

The current study examines the knowledge of three pairs of student teachers and their mentors, within one educational setting, a middle school with a level of available technology which, while substantial enough to merit observation, was not so high as to be atypical. To study this setting, we spent more than three months and conducted eighteen interviews. While our results are instructive, we see several avenues for making this line of research more generative.

First, the current study did not attempt to identify experts. The mentor and student teachers we describe here were not selected based on their expertise and we made no formal judgments about whether or not they were experts either in their content domains or in the use of educational technology. Future research may seek to determine whether the knowledge of experts differs from that of non-experts, as well as whether expert knowledge is more advantageous in suggesting courses of action for teachers and teacher educators.

In a similar vein, the current study was naturalistic. Participants were not selected by virtue of any reform-oriented interventions being instantiated in their classrooms, nor were they necessarily encouraged to adopt any particular curriculum or practices. Subsequent studies may seek to couple an educational reform approach with research into the nature of educational technology knowledge.

We had the luxury of studying this site for an extended period of time. As a graduate student and research fellow at the time of data collection, Margerum-Leys had the freedom to engage in research designs that might be impractical for a faculty member or full time educational researcher. Future modifications to the research methods employed here might lead to more efficient means of study while still yielding rich qualitative results.

Lastly, the number of participants in the current study was small and concentrated in a single school site. As an illustration of an important phenomenon, we do not feel that the study's small size was a fatal shortcoming. Still, increasing the number of cases to be studied in future research might afford a wider set of descriptions that could in turn be of more benefit to the field.

DISCUSSION

The use of an explanatory theory—components drawn from Shulman's (1987) general model of teacher knowledge—as an organizing framework offers a means of dealing with the inherent complexity of case data. By illuminating sections of the data that were especially well aligned with the theoretical model, the narratives related in this chapter provide the reader with text that reflects the underlying complexity of case study data while furnishing comprehensible results. The particular episodes presented here populate a structure that gives evidence that knowledge of educational technology dwells and flows along the same lines as other teacher knowledge. This has implications for teacher development and preparation that are discussed in the subsections below.

Implications for Teacher Preparation in Educational Technology

Teacher preparation in educational technology has traditionally focused on either stand-alone university coursework or technology infused into teacher education courses such as educational psychology or teaching methods (Willis & Mehlinger, 1996). However, the student teaching placement is a source of pedagogical knowledge and a site for exploring mentoring relationships (Easdown, 1994). As pre-service teachers move into their student teaching placements, attention should be paid to the technology available in those placements and to intentionally linking university preparation with the opportunities which students are likely to encounter. This is in line with constructivist principles of teacher education. Richardson (1997) observes that constructivism describes not how teacher education students *should* learn but in fact how they *do* learn. Meaning is constructed based on the intersection between learners' existing knowledge and their experiences. From the standpoint of acquiring knowledge of educational technology, a constructivist perspective would argue that opportunities for authentic experiences are a necessary condition for learning to occur.

Implications for Professional Development

In general, professional development in educational technology lacks an empirical or theoretical basis and is in need of a more theoretically grounded approach (Fishman et al., in press). While this study was not a professional development effort per se, the participants made mutual gains in educational technology knowledge and the mentor teachers unanimously felt that our work together constituted professional development for them. By being situated entirely in context, the work of the student teachers, mentor teachers, and Margerum-Leys together was pedagogically aligned with the teaching goals of Monroe Middle School's written and enacted curricula. Both longer timeframe and awareness of classroom context are useful for professional development (Cognition and Technology Group at Vanderbilt, 1996). Viewing student teachers as professional development partners gives the opportunity for extended contact and immersion in context.

CONCLUSION

With the rise in access to and emphasis on technology in the schools, student teachers have both an opportunity and an obligation to acquire knowledge about technology's role in teaching and learning. The knowledge that they can acquire in the field has traditionally been difficult for teacher preparation programs to help them to acquire during the coursework phase of their teacher education program. Our results indicate that while university coursework is useful for acquiring content knowledge, pedagogical knowledge and pedagogical content knowledge are more readily acquired within the teaching context.

Understanding how knowledge is acquired in particular field placements can help university teacher preparation programs to make the process of teacher education more explicit and better integrated with learning experiences available at the university. Through awareness of the teaching and technology issues which students may face, teacher preparation programs may be able to better structure their program.

As teacher education students have an obligation to acquire knowledge of educational technology, teacher educators have an obligation to understand the opportunities available to their students and to weave together knowledge acquired in field settings with their experiences at the university. Certain essential educational technology knowledge may be difficult to acquire in the classroom setting; an awareness of the complexity of educational technology knowledge and the mechanisms through which it is acquired can be valuable for teacher educators.

In the learning process, both student teachers and their mentors have much to offer each other. Among other positive contributions, student teachers bring with them current content knowledge of technology. This knowledge has been acquired through their own life habits as members of a generation that takes computer technology for granted. Additionally, student teachers introduce content knowledge that they have acquired through their university preparation.

Mentor teachers serve as pedagogical guides in the process of instantiating educational technology content knowledge and of acquiring educational technology pedagogical and pedagogical content knowledge. Mentor teachers have a deep, situated knowledge of students and their learning needs. This knowledge helps them to understand the pedagogical implications of technology use and in turn to help student teachers to understand these implications. Additionally, mentor teachers may have content knowledge that is more directly applicable to teaching and learning with technology. Coburn (1999) notes the importance of mentors for professional development in educational technology. Mentor teachers in this study provided the benefits of mentoring for their student teachers, aiding them directly and indirectly in learning about the use of educational technology.

The university plays a role in this process of sharing knowledge between mentor and student teachers. Seeding relevant content knowledge in coursework helps the student teachers to have knowledge to offer in their field placements. Developing educational technology knowledge in mentor teachers assures that student teachers will have a productive environment for learning. Through research such as the present study, we hope to bring to teacher education an understanding of the importance of a broad conception of educational technology knowledge. Further, we believe that teacher education programs can profit by long term relationships between university and field settings, using those relationships to further content and pedagogical knowledge. Understanding the nature of educational technology knowledge and its acquisition is key to meeting the demand for new teachers who can enter the field with the ability to infuse technology into their teaching in ways which support student learning at a high level.

ACKNOWLEDGMENTS

This research was supported in part by a research training grant from the Spencer Foundation to the University of Michigan.

The authors gratefully acknowledge the constructive suggestions of Robert Seidman and an anonymous reviewer, as well as Barry Fishman, Fred Goodman, Bradford Orr, and Virginia Richardson, professors at the University of Michigan.

REFERENCES

Bogdan, R.C., & Biklen, S.K. (1992). *Qualitative research for education* (2nd ed.). Boston: Allyn and Bacon.

Borko, H., & Putnam, R.T. (1996). Learning to teach. In D.C. Berliner & R.C. Calfee (Eds.), *Handbook of educational psychology* (pp. 673–708). New York: Macmillan.

Carter, K. (1990). Teachers' knowledge and learning to teach. In W.R. Houston (Ed.), *Handbook of research on teacher education* (pp. 291–301). New York: Macmillan.

CEO Forum. (1997). *School technology and readiness (STaR) report: From pillars to progress* (Annual report). The CEO Forum.

Clandinin, D.J., & Connelly, F.M. (1996). Teachers' professional knowledge landscapes: Teacher stories—Stories of teachers—School stories—Stories of schools. *Educational Researcher, 25*(3), 24–30.

Coburn, J. (1999). Teachers become technology students—to become better teachers. *School Planning and Management, 38*(3), 38–40.

Cochran-Smith, M., Garfield, E., & Greenberger, R. (1992). Student teachers and their teacher: Talking our way into new understandings. In N.A. Branscombe, D. Goswami, & J. Schwartz (Eds.), *Students teaching, teachers learning* (pp. 274–292). Portsmouth, NH: Boynton/Cook Heinemann.

Cochran-Smith, M., & Lytle, S.L. (1999). Relationships of knowledge and practice: Teacher learning in communities. In A. Iran-Nejad & P.D. Pearson (Eds.), *Review of research in education* (Vol. 24, pp. 249–306). Washington, DC: American Educational Research Association.

Cognition and Technology Group at Vanderbilt. (1996). Looking at technology in context: A framework for understanding technology and education research. In D.C. Berliner & R.C. Calfee (Eds.), *Handbook of educational psychology* (pp. 807–840). New York: Macmillan.

Connelly, F.M., & Clandinin, D.J. (1995). Personal and professional knowledge landscapes: A matrix of relations. In F.M. Connelly & D.J. Clandinin (Eds.), *Teachers' professional knowledge landscapes* (Vol. 15, pp. 25–35). New York: Teachers College Press.

Easdown, G. (1994). Student teachers, mentors, and information technology. *Journal of Information Technology for Teacher Education, 3*(1), 63–78.

Emerson, R.M., Fretz, R.I., & Shaw, L.L. (1995). *Writing ethnographic fieldnotes.* Chicago: The University of Chicago Press.

Fenstermacher, G.D. (1994). The knower and the known: The nature of knowledge in research on teaching. In L. Darling-Hammond (Ed.), *Review of research in education* (Vol. 20, pp. 3–56). Washington, DC: American Educational Research Association.

Fishman, B., Marx, R.W., Best, S., & Tal, R. (in press). Linking teacher and student learning to improve professional development in systemic reform. *Teaching and teacher education.*

Gibson, I.W., & King, S. (1997, July 6–8). *Partnerships, technology and teaching: Celebrating the link between universities and rural communities.* Paper presented at the National Conference for the Society for Provision of Education in Rural Australia, Adelaide, South Australia.

Greeno, J.G. (1998). The situativity of knowing, learning, and research. *American Psychologist, 53*(1), 5–26.

Grossman, P.L. (1990). *The making of a teacher: Teacher knowledge and teacher education.* New York: Teachers College Press.

Handler, M.G. (1993). Preparing new teachers to use computer technology: Perceptions and suggestions for teacher educators. *Computers and Education, 20*(2), 147–156.

Krajcik, J., Soloway, E., Blumenfeld, P., & Marx, R. (1998). Scaffolded technology tools to promote teaching and learning in science. In C. Dede (Ed.), *ASCD yearbook 1998: Learning with technology* (pp. 31–46). Alexandria, VA: The Association for Supervision and Curriculum Development.

Margerum-Leys, J. (1999). *Teacher knowledge and educational technology: A conceptual mapping.* Ann Arbor: The University of Michigan.

Means, B., & Olson, K. (1995). *Technology's role in education reform: Findings from a national study of innovating schools.* Menlo Park, CA: SRI International.

Putnam, R.T., & Borko, H. (2000). What do new views of knowledge and thinking have to say about research on teacher learning? *Educational Researcher, 29*(1), 4–16.

President's Committee of Advisors on Science and Technology Panel on Educational Technology. (1997). *Report to the president on the use of technology to strengthen k–12 education in the United States* Washington, DC: Executive office of the President of the United States.

Richardson, V. (1997). Constructivist teaching and teacher education: Theory and practice. In V. Richardson (Ed.), *Constructivist teacher education: Building a world of new understandings* (pp. 3–14). London: The Falmer Press.

Seidman, I.E. (1991). *Interviewing as qualitative research.* New York: Teachers College Press.

Shulman, L.S. (1987). Knowledge and teaching: Foundations of the new reform. *Harvard Educational Review, 57*(1), 1–22.

Tatel, E.S. (1996). Improving classroom practice: Ways experienced teachers change after supervising student teachers. In M.W. McLaughlin & I. Oberman (Eds.), *Teacher learning: New policies, new practices* (pp. 252). New York: Teachers College.

Wenglinsky, H. (1998). *Does it compute? The relationship between educational technology and studen achievement in mathematics.* Educational Testing ServiceETS).

Willis, J., & Mehlinger, H.D. (1996). Information technology and teacher education. In J. Sikula (Ed.), *Handbook of research on teacher education* (2nd ed., pp. 978–1029). New York: Simon & Schuster Macmillan.

Wilson, S.M.,& Berne, J. (1999). Teacher learning and the acquisition of professional knowledge: An examination of research on contemporary professional development. In A. Iran-Nejad & P.D. Pearson (Eds.), *Review of research in education* (Vol. 24, pp. 172–210). Washington, DC: American Educational Research Association.

Yin, R.K. (1984/1989). *Case study research: Design and methods* (rev. ed., Vol. 5). Newbury Park, CA: Sage Publications.

Yin, R.K. (1993). *Applications of case study research* (paperback ed., Vol. 34). Thousand Oaks, CA: Sage.

ABOUT THE CONTRIBUTORS

Tom Bird, Associate Professor of Teacher Education at Michigan State University, recently completed a term as Assistant Chairperson of that department. He teaches a course on classroom management and lesson planning for elementary teacher candidates, in which he has been attempting to integrate intelligent uses of information technology.

Bertram (Chip) Bruce is a Professor of Library and Information Science at the University of Illinois at Urbana-Champaign. He has published extensively on educational uses of technology. His recent books include *Network-based classrooms: Promises and realities* and *Electronic Quills: A situated evaluation of using computers for writing in classrooms.* He is also the host of the monthly Technology Department in the *Journal of Adolescent and Adult Literacy.*

Paul Conway is a College Lecturer in the Education Department at the National University of Ireland, Cork and during the summer is a Visiting Professor of Educational Psychology at Michigan State University where he teaches on the MA in Teaching and Learning with Technology program. He is currently Co-Editor of the journal "Irish Educational Studies." His research interests are in teacher learning, technology policy, and socio-cultural perspectives on learning. Prior to returning to Ireland, he was an Assistant Professor of Educational Psychology and Human Development at Cleveland State University.

Cindy Kendall taught high school Spanish for 15 years and is currently at Michigan State University completing her doctorate in Curriculum, Teaching and Educational Policy. Cindy also works extensively with K–16 educa-

What Should Teachers Know About Technology?: Perspectives and Practices, pages 161–164
Copyright © 2003 by Information Age Publishing
All rights of reproduction in any form reserved.

tors on integrating technology into teaching and learning, as an instructor at the National K–12 Foreign Language Resource Center at Iowa State University. As the President of the Michigan Foreign Language Association, Cindy is an advocate for K–16 world language instruction and collaborates with state and national leaders on issues regarding technology and professional development for practicing second language educators.

Matthew J. Koehler is an assistant professor at Michigan State University. He received his Ph.D. in 1999 in Educational Psychology from the University of Wisconsin. His research interests include the design of hypermedia and video cases to facilitate teacher learning, and methods of developing technological literacy through innovate design-based activities.

Jim Levin is a Professor of Educational Psychology, and a Faculty Affiliate at the Beckman Institute for Advanced Science and Technology, at the University of Illinois at Urbana-Champaign. His research focuses on finding ways to improve problem solving through collaborative interaction through networks, and to help people learn to be better problem solvers by providing powerful distributed learning environments. He has developed several innovative models of learning, including the concept of teleapprenticeships. He has recently been studying "teaching teleapprenticeships", instructional frameworks that allow education students to learn within the context of remote K–12 classrooms. He has been exploring ways to use advanced technologies to improve education, locally, nationally, and internationally.

Jon Margerum-Leys is an assistant professor of educational technology at Eastern Michigan University. His work focuses on the knowledge base for teaching with technology and the formation and dissemination of that knowledge in K–12 settings. The chapter in this volume is drawn from Jon's University of Michigan dissertation, which was awarded the 2002 Outstanding Dissertation Award by the American Association of Colleges for Teacher Education.

Ronald W. Marx, Ph.D. Stanford University, is an educational psychologist focusing on how to help teachers engage their students in thoughtful learning of science. Along with University of Michigan colleagues in the School of Education, the College of Engineering and the School of Public Health, he has formed the Center for Highly Interactive Computing in Education (hi-ce). With funding from the National Science Foundation, the Department of Education, and the Spencer, Kellogg, and Joyce Foundations, hi-ce has embarked on an ambitious program of research and development in collaboration with school districts (most notably the Detroit Public Schools), to promote standards-based systemic reform in science education. This work investigates a range of critical issues in reform across five dimensions of study—curriculum and pedagogy, technology design and development, teacher professional development, community engagement, and policy and management. Dr. Marx is currently serving as the Co-Director of the NSF Center for Learning Technologies in Urban Schools.

Punyashloke Mishra is assistant professor of Technology and Education in the department of Learning, Technology, and Culture, and a Research Associate with the Media Interface and Network Design (MIND) Lab. He has an undergraduate degree in Electrical Engineering, Masters' degrees in Visual and Mass Communications, and a Ph.D. in Educational Psychology. His research has focused on the psychological and social aspects related to the design and use of computer-based learning environments. His other interests include online learning, visual literacy, and creativity.

Cheryl L. Rosaen is Associate Professor of Teacher Education and a faculty Team Leader in Michigan State University's five-year Teacher Preparation Program. She teaches courses in integrated, literature-based teaching and learning of English language arts in culturally diverse classrooms, learning to teach in school settings, and the curriculum and pedagogy of teacher education. For over 10 years, Dr. Rosaen has participated in collaborative work with elementary teachers where she conducts research on language and literacy learning and learning to teach, while also collaborating with classroom teachers in improving their curriculum and teaching. In addition, she conducts research on learning to teach in the Teacher Preparation Program, with an emphasis on understanding the role technology can play in supporting pre-service teacher learning.

Sophia Hueyshan Tan is a doctoral candidate at College of Education, Michigan State University. Her research interests include social networks, online distance learning, and technology and teacher education. She has published articles and presented at professional conferences about computer literacy and children, online writing, and distance learning.

Mark Urban-Lurain, Ph.D., Educational Psychology, Michigan State University, is the Director of Research and Development for Instructional Technology in the Division of Science and Math Education at Michigan State University. Over the past 15 years, he and Dr. Donald Weinshank have designed several large enrollment computer science courses using a wide variety of instructional technologies. Mark's research interests are in cognition and technology, performance-based assessments, modeling how novices learn with and about computers, and the implications of this research for teaching practice

Yong Zhao is an associate professor of educational psychology with interests in teacher adoption of technology, technology diffusions in schools, and web-based learning environments. He also directs the Center for Teaching and Technology. His research activities focus on the social, cultural and psychological interactions between technology and education. His current research projects include a social constructivist analysis of technology adoption in schools, exploring the interactions between teachers and technology, and examining the cognitive and affective effects of computer-mediated learning communities.